CRAIGSLIST
CONFESSIONAL

CRAIGSLIST CONFESSIONAL

A COLLECTION OF SECRETS FROM ANONYMOUS STRANGERS

HELENA DEA BALA

GALLERY BOOKS

New York   London   Toronto   Sydney   New Delhi

Gallery Books
An Imprint of Simon & Schuster, Inc.
1230 Avenue of the Americas
New York, NY 10020

First Gallery Books hardcover edition July 2020

GALLERY BOOKS and colophon are registered trademarks
of Simon & Schuster, Inc.

For information about special discounts for bulk purchases,
please contact Simon & Schuster Special Sales at 1-866-506-1949
or business@simonandschuster.com.

The Simon & Schuster Speakers Bureau can bring authors to your live event. For
more information or to book an event, contact the Simon & Schuster Speakers
Bureau at 1-866-248-3049 or visit our website at www.simonspeakers.com.

Interior design by Davina Mock-Maniscalco

Manufactured in the United States of America

10   9   8   7   6   5   4   3   2   1

Library of Congress Cataloging-in-Publication Data

Names: Bala, Helena Dea, author.
Title: Craigslist confessional : a collection of secrets from anonymous
strangers / Helena Dea Bala.
Identifiers: LCCN 2019047888 (print) | LCCN 2019047889 (ebook) |
ISBN 9781982114961 (hardcover) | ISBN 9781982114985 (ebook)
Subjects: LCSH: Self-disclosure—Case studies. | Interpersonal communication.
| Interpersonal relations.
Classification: LCC BF697.5.S427 B347 2020 (print) |
LCC BF697.5.S427 (ebook) | DDC 158—dc23
LC record available at https://lccn.loc.gov/2019047888
LC ebook record available at https://lccn.loc.gov/2019047889

ISBN 978-1-9821-1496-1
ISBN 978-1-9821-1498-5 (ebook)

To Alex, who kept me going.
To Ronan, may you have courage and kindness in spades.
And to the people who have shared their lives with me—thank you.

Contents

IDENTITY

FAMILY

Introduction

For the past five years, I've listened to strangers I've met on Craigslist tell me stories they've never told anyone before. I interviewed someone who went through gender-reassignment surgery and fell in love for the very first time, as his true self. I spoke with a man who lost his wife to alcoholism and struggled to rebuild his life without her. I cried when I listened to a veteran who lost both of his legs after serving two tours of combat abroad. I spoke to a woman who detailed her life as a former Jehovah's Witness and to a Mormon faced with telling his family that he is gay.

In these five years, I've heard stories about sexual abuse and mental illness, divorce and death, addiction and disability—stories that have left me in awe at the breadth and depth of humanity, at our ability to overcome and rebuild, forgive and move on, heal and give back. I've learned to listen, to bear witness to heartbreaking loss and regret, to provide a safe outlet for healing. In this climate, where diversity is simultaneously celebrated and used to monger fear, judgment, and separatism, I've learned above all else that pain, in its protean forms, can unite us as human beings—that each of us can be a light when someone's day feels particularly dark.

Before I started *Craigslist Confessional*, I worked as a lobbyist out of a tiny office in downtown Washington, DC. I stressed out over deadlines, client meetings, unanswered emails, and office politics. I purposefully distracted myself with daily minutiae so as not to let my unhappiness fully settle in. I'd always wanted to have a job where I helped people. But somewhere along the way, I got sidetracked. My work left me empty. Showing up every day to do something when my heart wasn't in it felt like living in a perpetual existential crisis.

Nothing made things more painful than being isolated, unable to share my feelings. I felt alienated, invisible, misunderstood, dismissed, and shut out. I was locked into a life of indentured servitude to my student loan provider. As an immigrant, I'd worked hard to finally win my American dream, only to find a mirage in its place—an experience very different from what I'd expected.

But I didn't feel entitled to complain. Each day on my way to work, I passed at least five homeless people and reminded myself: *You have it good. You are employed. You are educated. You are healthy. You have so much more than most people.* So I shamed myself into a disquiet silence.

To convince others—especially my parents, who had sacrificed so much for my happiness and success—that everything was going perfectly well, I curated my life and presented only the happiest, most perfect parts of it for others to see. Social media filters and reality television fed me "real" versions of people I was meant to emulate—successful, attractive, healthy, and rich adults leading travel-filled and meaningful lives free of the drudgery of everydayness.

More and more, the pressure to keep up appearances made me feel inadequate and lonely. The dissonance between my reality and the person I presented to the world was so jarring. I felt inherently dishonest. And, I often thought, if I couldn't be honest with others, how could I be honest with myself? Had I gotten so warped, so sucked into playing the role of the perfect daughter, the perfect employee, the perfect girlfriend, that I could no longer tell my genuine life from the one I was projecting?

One day, as I was walking back to work from Capitol Hill, I spotted Joe, a homeless man who panhandled in front of the office building. I could almost always count on seeing him standing in the same spot, day after day, shaking a paper cup and wearing a black tattered shirt. Whenever I could, I brought him boxed lunches that I'd pick up during Hill briefings and got him the occasional snack or drink. I had a particular soft spot for Joe because of a bitter memory from my first day of work. Two young security guards had been checking me in when one of them excused himself. He went outside to talk to Joe—I was only able to catch a few words from the exchange, but the gist was that the guards had received complaints from the building's occupants about Joe's panhandling and he should move along elsewhere. Joe nodded his head slowly, but he stood his ground as if to protest the unfairness.

It broke my heart.

"Are you upset with me?" Joe asked, wondering why I'd rounded the corner lunchless.

The truth was that I was broke. My salary at the lobbying firm was laughable—law grads are a dime a dozen in DC, and we're cheap and replaceable, especially at the entry level—and between student loans, rent, and food, I was struggling to make ends meet.

Joe looked sad as I mumbled a half-hearted explanation. I blinked back tears and asked if it was all right to spend time with him and talk that day. I went around the corner and got a sandwich to share, and we sat next to each other. I asked him about how he'd become homeless. Did he have any family? Where did he stay when the weather was bad? Did he often go hungry? He answered my questions with intense detail, often stumbling over his words.

Then he asked me about my job and my life. I surprised myself with what I shared—thoughts that had, until then, seemed so personal and devastating but paled in comparison to Joe's everyday struggle. For the first time I was able to be refreshingly honest. I spoke without fear that he'd judge me or that the gossip would trickle down to friends, family, and coworkers. Neither of us had anything to gain from the other. Ours was an interaction born out of need. It felt, simply, like we were confessing.

Joe listened patiently, seeming grateful to have someone to talk to. And as I watched him shake his cup of change at passersby while we talked, I understood why. Sometimes people shot him dirty looks. Sometimes they tossed him a handful of change, maybe a flickering look of judgment—or was it shame, fear, guilt?—but mostly people completely ignored him: no friendly smiles, no inquisitive glances. He was totally invisible.

"Very few people," he told me, "treat me like I'm a human being."

That's when *Craigslist Confessional* was born. It is a project about hearing and seeing what others don't—about pulling back the curtain that separates our secretive inner lives from our perfectly curated outer lives. My "job" is to listen when no one else will. I do it for free—and completely anonymously.

Inspired by my talk with Joe, I posted an ad in the Craigslist personals section. "Tell me about yourself," the subject line read.

I'm not certain what I hoped to accomplish with the ad. The truth is that I didn't have a grand plan. Yes, I wanted to put something good out in the world. I wanted to help people by listening to them—by giving them a place to be themselves. But if I'm honest, I also wanted to be heard and seen, too. I wanted to not feel alone. I wanted to connect with people beyond the superficial—I wanted our common struggle to unite us in a way that felt *real*. So posting the ad was an ill-thought-out attempt at trying to replicate that connection with Joe, and I really didn't think much would come of it.

But I was *so very wrong*. Over the next few days, the responses came in nonstop. And what was more surprising was the fact that the ad seemed to have hit a nerve, because people were very willing to go out on a limb with me—to meet me over coffee and to talk.

My first meeting was at a Starbucks right across the street from work. I sat there for a half hour, nervously picking at my nail polish and becoming more convinced by the minute that the woman who'd emailed me wouldn't show. Then I saw someone walking hurriedly across the street, looking just as anxious as I felt, and my heart jumped—*Oh my God, she actually came.*

We made small talk as we waited in line to get two iced drinks, and then we walked to a nearby park, where she told me about her two-decades-long struggle with heroin addiction and the toll it had taken on her life, marriage, and children. It was surreal. I kept expecting to see all that she'd gone through written somewhere on her body. But physically she betrayed nothing. Her scarred arms were carefully hidden under long sleeves. Her nails were manicured; her hair perfectly coiffed.

At the end of our meeting, I offered to walk her to her Metro stop. She pointed out street corners where she'd scored smack many moons ago. Mostly, though, we were both quiet. I felt very emotional. I didn't know how to express to her how much it meant that she'd trusted me with her story. I didn't know how to explain that it would be safe with me. And so I hugged her, and then she got on the escalator and the underground started slowly erasing her—and she looked back at me and waved. And that was the last time I saw her.

When I got home that day, I responded to more emails—and then I kept going. I met people in person or spoke to them over the phone about anything they wanted to share. For many, it was the first time they'd been able to recount their stories without fear of stigma or ostracism.

"I've never said any of this out loud," people said, or "I haven't even told my therapist [or best friend, or family, or partner] about this."

Although it felt amazing to be able to do something for other people, ironing out the "interview" process was bumpy. Some things I got right from the start—others, very wrong. For one, I had no way of recognizing the people I was meeting. Henry, one of the first people I met with, sat next to me at a Starbucks for about twenty minutes before I realized he was the person who had responded to the ad. For a while, I started bringing a gray floppy hat to meetings with me so that I would be easy to pick out.

But that ease of recognition was also potentially scary. It's Craigslist, after all. Every person I told about what I was doing would invariably bring up the movie *The Craigslist Killer*. So it got me thinking that maybe I was putting a target on my back. I abandoned the hat in favor of having the subject describe what he/she was going to wear to the meeting. But I kept the coffee shop locale because it was public, familiar, and therefore it felt safe. For the first couple of months, Alex, my now husband, insisted on shadowing me to as many of my weekend meetings as he could. He would sit in the opposite corner of the shop and read a book, all the while keeping an eye out for me.

I didn't bring a notebook to the first few meetings because my aim hadn't been to write down these stories. I mostly listened, but the process was much more like a conversation. After each talk, I would get home and feel emotionally heavy, so I journaled about the experience to unburden myself. I noticed after several rounds of repeating this pattern—listen, get home, write to unburden—that it was cathartic for me to write about what I'd heard. It gave me distance from the experience, and clarity. I also often went back to read what I'd written. It felt like the stories had ripened over the time left unread, and they brought a new dimension to my understanding of what had been shared. I was realizing the value of putting these stories down on paper, and the aim of the project slowly unveiled itself: I wanted these stories to find a home, a kindred spirit who needed them. What if, by sharing the stories I heard, I could help other people going through something similar? What if the stories helped someone feel less lonely, or get a better understanding of a taboo topic, or spot someone in crisis? What if I could use my position— my luck in being someone privy to these outstanding stories—to pay it forward?

I amended my original Craigslist ad to include a plan: I wanted to write these stories down and hopefully, some day, publish them. I reached back out to a couple of the first subjects, whom I'd met before I started writing, and got their permission to write about their stories, too. I started bringing a notebook to my meetings and taking notes. Regardless of the newfound purpose, the project was always, first and foremost, about listening—about creating space for others to share fearlessly, without reservation. Whether they wanted their stories to be written was up to them, and I always provided the option to just meet and talk, no notebook—off the record, so to speak.

Still, I feared that the note-taking, the prospect of having their stories published, might quash potential subjects' ability to be totally open. So I took many precautions to ensure total anonymity, and the venue—Craigslist—really helped. No real names. Scrambled email addresses. The subjects could share as little or as much as they wanted—they could test out their comfort level and boundaries without feeling like they had something on the line, like they might be exposed. To further ensure that they remained anonymous, I changed their names and, only where absolutely necessary and requested by the subject, other small details that might give their identity away—making sure, of course, that the change didn't affect any germane aspects of their story. Finally, I always gave the subject the option of requesting that I leave out information they felt might give away their identity.

Some of the precautions I took, over time, began to feel unnecessary. Although I continued to change names and otherwise protect anonymity, I found that people were willing to be open, to share their stories, in hopes that they might be some solace for someone in need. And I discovered, too, that people *needed* to talk. Not to converse, not to get advice, not to have clever repartee. They needed to get things off their chests. Truly, to vent. So the interviews went from a conversational style in the very beginning to very one-sided—about 95 percent them, 5 percent me. I listened. I asked occasional questions, mostly to clarify details. Maybe I asked a leading question or two (I am trained in law, after all), just to get to the heart of something. But for the most part, I wanted to create the impression that I was not there at all—that the person was talking to him- or herself, out loud. Even thoughts are transformed, filtered, when they're thought for an audience. I wanted very little of that filter, so I practiced listening. Just listening. Not thinking about how I was going to respond. Not interjecting. Not creating any sort of personal or emotional reaction to something shared—this was *very* hard—but just being present.

I don't think these meetings were a cure-all for my subjects. I hoped that they would be therapeutic but not *like therapy*. Therapy, for myriad reasons, just isn't available or an option for many people, so I did what I could to provide a listening ear, instead—*to not let the perfect be the enemy of the good*. When more was asked of me—more direction, more help—I put my subjects in touch with people who have the training to provide what they needed. I became comfortable in admitting when I was out of my depth, and I found that my lack of formal training was a plus—it allowed me to keep an open mind and an unprimed perspective. Ultimately, people were happy to have the opportunity to help others by telling their stories—we shared a vision in which each story would find a second self.

At the beginning of every conversation, I asked permission to take handwritten notes. When something struck me as very singularly and perfectly expressed, I took down direct quotes. Whenever possible, I also tried to stay true to the person's manner of speaking. The meetings themselves were very loosely structured—I'd introduce myself, give a quick recap of the project, ask for permission to write their stories, and then give the subjects a chance to ask questions. Then, I told them to "jump in wherever you feel comfortable." I noticed that asking people to tell me their stories gently nudged them into a different, somewhat more removed perspective into their own lives. The process of creating their own narrative gave them distance, but it also forced them to come up with a beginning, middle, and end—and that was the most beneficial aspect of this exercise.

The meetings are long—average meetings are about one and a half to two and a half hours, but my longest was eight hours!—and the flow of the interview was generally stream of consciousness (again, I was trying to create a safe and comfortable environment that made the subjects feel as if they'd granted me permission to listen in to their thoughts). The act of the subject's having to tell his or her story, however, gave the conversation structure, and it necessitated the need for an ending—so it got every person thinking, *How does my story end? How do I make the most of what has happened to me?*

After every conversation, I gave myself a maximum of one week from the date shared to write up the story. I wanted everything to be fresh in my memory so that the resulting story could be as faithful and accurate as possible. On a few occasions, I missed my self-imposed deadline. I found that I needed distance from some stories, that I quite simply couldn't bring myself to write them up. Some of them hit very close to home, so revisiting them was difficult. In some other cases—for example, the story of a father who admitted to sexually molesting his daughters when they were young girls, after their mother died from cancer—I found it impossible to suspend judgment, to be impartial, to write clearly. Other stories—ones about random misfortunes and senseless tragedies—those types of stories scared me.

But because I had found work that meant so much to me, I was eager to do it all the time. Every spare moment. When I took time to myself, I felt selfish. Perhaps the hardest lesson I had to learn throughout these past five years is that, in doing work like this, it was more important than ever to establish and honor my own boundaries, and to take care of my own mental health first. It very quickly became too much, and it started taking a toll. It somehow hadn't occurred to me that I would take all these stories so *very* personally, that I would feel so personally invested, personally wronged, personally hurt by what had happened to other people. I often felt overwhelmed and unable to see a silver lining—when you hear primarily about tragedy, sadness, injustice, and heartbreak every single day, it's easy to lose sight of what is good in the world. But when I began to lose faith in the project (*How can this make a difference when bad things happen to people every single day?*), or started to feel foolish and idealistic, I'd go to another meeting and, without fail, I was reminded that this was necessary—it was a service people needed, and I was lucky enough to be the one in a position to offer it.

A few months after I started taking these meetings, my parents called me from the road.

"We are coming to visit you for your birthday," my mom chirped. "We're on our way already!"

"But I have to work. I have a busy week," I said, trying to explain the demands of my schedule.

Eventually I gave up resistance: I'd have to take the day off from my lobbying job and cancel the few Craigslist meetings I had set up.

When they arrived, they insisted on seeing the building where I worked. I took them inside the lobby and introduced them to the guards. My parents looked small and out of place, and my mom's eyes welled up with tears.

"We are so proud of you, Helena," my mom said. "You must be so happy here. Take a photo of us!"

When I look at the snapshot of my parents grinning ear to ear in front of the building I hated going inside every day, I think about how much I hid from them. I couldn't tell them how unhappy I was because I didn't want to ruin their joy over my accomplishments. Inside, I was filled with anxieties shared by many first-generation immigrants and people my age. I felt that practical choices and financial stability were more important than taking risks and doing work that I valued and loved.

When we moved to this country from Albania, we were dirt-poor. I slept on a futon in the living room of our one-bedroom apartment from age thirteen to eighteen. My dad, a former ambassador, started working as a Barton security guard at the Home Depot. My mom—a former doctor—was cleaning houses to keep us afloat. I often came home from school and saw my mother crying.

"Don't worry, Mama. It will be okay," I would say, feeling the weight of my parents' sacrifices.

On the weekends, I tagged along and helped her. We would stop at Dunkin' Donuts, grab two medium coffees, share an egg-and-cheese croissant, and drive our beat-up 1985 Ford Tempo up the long driveways of Connecticut mansions.

"This is why you have to study hard. This is why we came to

this country," my mother would say as we busied ourselves washing, dusting, vacuuming, making beds, and taking out the trash.

"Do you think we'll ever have a house of our own?" she'd ask every now and again, usually as she was scrubbing ferociously, elbow-deep in someone else's bathtub.

"Of course, Mama," I'd say, planning out the future in my mind. When I grew up, I would get my parents their own little house. I would make sure my mom never cried again and that my dad never stressed over bills. I would justify everything they'd gone through.

But when I finally did "make it" as a lawyer, I didn't know which loan or bill to pay off first. I worked long hours, and I barely got to see my parents at all. Our nightly phone calls became shorter and shorter. Still, I sent them photos of my office that they shared with anyone and everyone, beaming with pride over their only daughter.

The unhappier I became, the more I searched in others' faces for a glimpse of my own feelings. But I saw only the well-guarded facades of people who had been taught the same things I had: be ambitious, be successful, be happy, be tough. And so, when we celebrated my birthday at dinner that night, I didn't tell my parents about my Craigslist meetings. I didn't tell them how unhappy I was at work, either. I am smiling in all the photos that we took that night, and what's really surprising is that I *look* happy.

I went in to work the next day, and I got called to the boss's office. Taking the day off, especially on short notice, was "discouraged" at work. Even though I'd tied up all the loose ends, he wasn't happy. The head of HR was there, too. I made little effort to do any damage control. In fact, the timing felt perfect. I'd spent many sleepless nights discussing my job with Alex. When the Craigslist meetings took off, I was doing as many as five or six a week, plus a full-time job. I was so taken by my side project that I had escapist daydreams about quitting my "real" job and just taking meetings. Alex and I had discussed things loosely—a plan of attack on the very off chance that I'd have the opportunity to focus on the meetings full-time. As I sat in front of HR and my boss, I had a "now or never" sort of moment. Somehow the conversation turned to my "not seeming happy" there, and I didn't contradict them. Before I knew it, I was telling them that I didn't think the job was a good fit. I felt that my position there had been misrepresented and that the salary was criminal. In short, I quit. My boss seemed surprised—was I sure? Did I want to stay on for an extra two weeks to give it another chance and reconsider? On the spot, I decided against it. I took two weeks' pay and secured a positive recommendation for a future employer, and I went back to my office.

Before I'd had a chance to process what had happened, the HR director knocked on my door and handed me a couple of empty boxes.

"If you don't want to pack right now, you can arrange it with me to come by and pick up your personal belongings this weekend," she said. I decided I'd had enough anxiety for the day, so I packed my bag and walked out of the building. Truth be told, I felt a little triumphant. It was a beautiful day. Things seemed very hopeful. Mostly, I was excited to get to work with the Craigslist meetings. I had this overwhelming feeling that I was sitting on something so much bigger than myself and that I owed it to my subjects to see it through.

I was walking in the direction of home, past the fire station on Thirteenth and L Streets in DC. Lost in thought, I didn't notice the commotion as a fire truck prepared to leave the station. I stepped in its way, and the driver laid on the horn, blasting me out of my thoughts and into reality: *Holy shit. I just quit my job.* I called Alex, sobbing.

It took a little while to get into the swing of things. Depending on how the ads did and how many I posted, I probably took a maximum of ten meetings a week. There were slow weeks during which I chose to focus on writing. But my goal was to give the Craigslist meetings my all for a year. That's it. One year of listening. I didn't try to get the word out, and I didn't try to get the stories published. I didn't want to think too far down the road, to clutter my head with preoccupations about monetizing my passion, legitimizing it to others—although of course the pressure was always there. But for the first year, my goal was to do something in service of others. I had a little bit of money saved; I deferred my loans, and I opened up a credit card. With Alex's blessing, I dove in.

The time went by incredibly quickly. Alex saw me through countless crises—low points during which I questioned my sanity. *What was I thinking?* Usually, they were triggered by conversations with well-meaning friends and acquaintances who just couldn't understand why I'd quit a perfectly good job to listen to people complain about their problems. *Isn't that what therapy is for? And you do it for free?*

It would have been intolerable to field these questions from my parents, so I decided not to tell them. For a little over a year, my parents were under the impression that their daughter was still blissfully working away as a lobbyist. I finally did tell them when Alex and I decided to move to New York. The move prompted a conversation about finding new employment, and I figured, *Well, now's as good a time as any.* My mother started crying, which I expected. And my father didn't speak to me for a year, which, to be honest, I also expected. Their disappointment in me was palpable and heartbreaking.

When we moved to New York, Alex and I started talking about getting married. Of course we had no money. "Negative money," as we called it, because of the student loans. Three-quarters of our pooled income went to rent, and the rest was food. We didn't go out. We could afford zero luxuries. The burden of putting Alex through this for the sake of chasing down my passion started to become unbearable. It was supposed to have been one year, but one year was turning into two, and I wasn't slowing down.

The energy of New York City gave me courage, though. Within a month of moving here, I'd decided that it was high time to find these stories a home. So I pitched my story as a listener to *Quartz* and Paul Smalera, the Ideas editor there, agreed to publish it. It did incredibly well for them, and I gathered up the gumption to pitch him a column, Craigslist Confessional. He made no promises but agreed to run a few stories and see how they did. The stories ended up having a home on *Quartz* for almost two years—an incredible run during which they found an audience beyond my wildest dreams. Posting on Craigslist became unnecessary—people were coming to *me* to share. Not only that, but they were reaching out to become listeners—*any advice on replicating what you're doing?* I felt, finally, like I had created the community I was looking for when I started this project—like maybe I wasn't so crazy to do this, after all.

Alex and I did end up getting married. We went to city hall, and the license cost us $35—affordable even by our standards. We also adopted a dog, Stanley Zbornak, and New York very quickly started to feel like home. I was writing and taking meetings constantly—things were looking up.

In January 2017, I was in our living room, scrolling through my news feed, when an article in the *Washington Post* stopped me in my tracks. It was about that winter's first homeless casualty in DC. The article, written by Julie Zauzmer, identified Joseph Watkins, also known as "the Cigarette man," as the man who had passed away on a park bench at the age of fifty-four.

"They found him on the park bench. My brother died on the park bench," Denise Watkins, Joe's sister, had told the reporter. "That's kind of sad. He was a good soul, you know."

Could Denise be the sister Joe had mentioned in our conversation? My heartbeat quickened as I read other details that coincided with what I knew about him—"He was easily distracted, irritable at the merest provocation and prone to rambling [. . .] He couldn't keep a job. Eventually he was diagnosed with schizophrenia." This was true of my Joe, too.

But I kept scrolling through the page, not wanting to believe it, looking for anything that could convince me otherwise. The article quoted a police report that had listed Joe at six foot three and 418 pounds. I remembered him as a slightly-above-average-size man. Frantically, I looked up his name on Google Images, but nothing came up. That night, at around 4:00 a.m., I awoke with a start and groggily pulled up the article again, taking down Julie's name and email address. The next day, I reached out to her.

Her response worried me. She hadn't been able to track down a photo of Joe, but most of our details—with some exceptions—matched up.

Could the article be referring to the same person? The question bothered me for months. I called up an old friend and told him I was planning on visiting DC. He offered up his couch, and I took the bus from New York to Union Station and hopped on the Red line to Metro Center. I walked past my old building and then to the park nearby. I looked for Joe as I did every time I walked down those streets; he wasn't there.

I often think about him and the effect that he has had on my life. I never had a chance to thank him for listening to me that day, and for letting me listen to him. I felt seen and heard for the first time in so long, and I hope I was able to make him feel the same. I wonder, too, what would have happened had I never stopped to talk to him. I would likely still be working in DC. I might have even been happy, who knows? But I would have missed out on meeting and speaking to hundreds of people who have changed my life, who have opened my heart wide and informed the person I am today.

So, to Joe and all the invisible people who've honored me by letting me see them, as they are—vulnerable, raw, afraid, honest, imperfect, and beautiful—*thank you*. My wish, in return, is that their stories will give you hope, perspective, and closure when you need it. I hope they'll bring you peace and allow you to open your heart to others with burdens of their own.

LOVE

Edie, sixties

I had a very typical pregnancy. We went to all the visits when my daughter was in utero—standard stuff—and everything checked out. Of course, this was 1980, so technology wasn't as advanced as it is these days. . . .

My daughter was born without complications, and she was a dream baby. I was so happy to have her, although I do remember that the first couple of months as a new mom were challenging, much more so than anyone will honestly tell you. I took Laura to the pediatrician for her two-month checkup, and I remember that he was listening to her heart with a stethoscope for an extra-long time.

I asked him, "Is everything all right?"

And he said, "Oh, yeah."

And we moved on.

I didn't think about the visit again. I was busy raising her, busy being the best mom I could be. I poured all my love and dedication into this little baby. She was a marvel. We couldn't believe she had come from us. My husband and I would spend hours after she went to sleep just talking about the new things she'd done that day—her personality, her mannerisms. She was decidedly, even then, herself.

Her fifteen-month checkup came around, and her pediatrician did the standard testing but again listened to her heart for a beat too long.

And he finally said, "I hear a bit of a heart murmur, but it could be significant or nonsignificant. I'm going to send you to a pediatric heart specialist, and we can go from there."

My intuition told me that it was going to be something—not in a fatalistic way. I just knew, though. I knew that something was wrong.

The specialist asked a few questions and then ordered an ECG, which conclusively told us that she had a heart defect—"a cluster of defects," they called it. One of the defects, he explained, could cause high blood pressure. The options he gave us were open-heart surgery or medication. Of course, surgery was risky. Medication might be effective, but who knows for how long, or it might not do much at all.

My husband wasn't there with me, and cell phones weren't around, either, so I drove to a gas station and used the pay phone to call my husband and tell him what the doctor had said. Now, I'm a very action-oriented person. When something is "wrong," I jump in to fix it. That's my defense mechanism. And I just didn't give myself a second to feel any kind of way about the news we'd gotten. I just sprang to action.

I sought a second opinion from a university hospital, and the pediatric heart specialist recommended surgery for two of the defects in the "cluster." And because I wanted nothing but the best, we also saw a world-renowned specialist who diagnosed Laura with Shone's syndrome and recommended surgery for three of the defects—coarctation of the aorta, double orifice mitral valve, and something else. I can't quite remember.

You know, it's funny, back in those days all of these fancy medical terms slid off my tongue like *I* was the pediatric heart surgeon. I read so much that I guess you might even say I knew more about my baby's heart than the average internist would. But I guess time fades things, even the suffering I thought would be etched into my bones forever.

We elected to have the aorta treated first because it was the most pressing issue. I read a book to Laura about surgery—it had these illustrations of the doctors wearing masks. Each time I would read it to her, I'd ask her what they were wearing, and she would exclaim, "Masks!" I would start giggling, and she followed suit. I wanted to show her that it wasn't scary—that she would be okay. Even though my heart ached, I couldn't let her sense my fear.

When they wheeled her away the day of her surgery, I didn't know if I'd ever see my child again. My mind raced. I begged God that she be safe. The whole family was terrified and trying to keep it together. At most hospitals, they tell you what to be prepared for after the surgery is over: lots of tubes, tape, needles, and masks. They tell you not to be alarmed. But my two-year-old just went in for open-heart surgery. *Alarmed* doesn't quite cover it.

After the surgery, the doctors told me that she had looked at them before they put her under and started giggling. My brave baby. She came out of the surgery with two pretty significant scars—one started on her spine, curved under the armpit, and ended under her breast; the other went down the center of her chest. And let me tell you, the pain you feel when you see your child like that—this perfect creation that you housed in your body and soul for nine months, that you brought into this world through tears and pain, that is the personified sum of the life-affirming love that you feel for another person—it is obliterating.

They told us, once we were discharged, that Laura wouldn't need to be on medication. But we went in for regular checkups every few months, and we took it crisis by crisis. It would be: "Okay, here's the crisis. You got through it. Now it's over. When is the next one coming?"

I was a person who needed to know the facts—the reality—through all of it. I needed to know what they would do to her, what the risks were . . . everything.

My husband looked at me one night and he said, "I can't do that." Meaning, *I can't know everything. It's too much.*

And I said to him, "I understand. I'll do it."

He wasn't good with illness.

At three years old, Laura had a second open-heart surgery and was on a heart-lung machine. This surgery was to replace her mitral valve. They replaced it with an entirely mechanical one called a St. Jude valve. She would have to be on blood thinners for the rest of her life, they told us. It was a twelve-hour surgery. As a parent, twelve hours of your child under the knife is an eternity. The waiting room is where the trauma deepens because you start thinking to yourself, *We were so lucky the first time around. Can we be that lucky again?*

Laura was part of a pioneer group of children to have these surgeries. At that time, there were no older survivors who had gone through them. So as parents, we had no idea if we were doing right by our baby or not. We had no blueprint to follow. We just did the best we could with the information we had.

Part of that meant I had to plan for Laura's funeral when she went in that second time. The doctor was honest about the odds, and I just wanted to make a few arrangements ahead of time so that if anything happened, I wouldn't have to do everything under distress. I went to the funeral home, and I picked out the sweetest, happiest casket I could find. I called a florist and arranged for roses. We're Jewish and technically we don't "do" flowers for funerals, but Laura loved red roses, so I ordered them anyways.

I tried to talk to my mom during this time. I just wanted to say out loud to someone, "What if she dies?"

She looked at me and she said, "Don't even think that way."

She was angry with me that I could think such a thing. But this was real to me. I had to prepare myself.

But she survived, and life—improbably, it seemed—went on. I had another baby—a son with colic who needed to nurse at all times. I made it work. I would stay in the hospital overnight, in Laura's room, with the baby. I woke up one morning and the head nurse told me that I couldn't have the baby there overnight.

I said, "Please don't do this to me. It's not his fault." I begged, but in the end, the answer was no. It was some sort of insurance liability issue. I ended up having to pump.

The hospital was filled with people like me, repeaters, who were there a lot. We knew the doctors and the nurses, and they became like family. There was one young nurse in particular, such a sweet soul, who wore these pink barrettes in her hair. She had very

thin hair, so the barrettes were for kids, and all the pediatric pa-
tients would tease her about them. Laura went in for an X-ray one
day, and the nurse was there.

I asked her, "How are you doing?"

And she kind of sighed and said, "You know, Edie, I've gotta tell
you. I have cancer. I'm dying."

And she did, she passed away. I wanted to do something for her,
so I started a scholarship fund at the hospital in her name. Her parents contacted me to thank me, and I told them, "I'll never forget
your daughter and everything she did for my daughter." Her parents
are ninety-eight and ninety-six now. I talk to them three times a
year, for birthdays and holidays.

A couple of years after Laura's second surgery, her father and I
divorced. It was very friendly. But the heaviness of our situation got
to us. Her valve replacement held tight until she was twelve, but
eventually she outgrew it and she needed another one. The doctor
said that they were going to get an adult woman's valve for the replacement, a size 27, that way Laura could grow into it and she
wouldn't need another surgery down the road.

But she developed a severe arrhythmia after the second replacement. The size 27 was too big for her, so we had to go in to
cardiovert her often—they would shock her heart back into a normal rhythm. We were in the hospital fifty-two times during her
twelfth year of life. Fifty-two. An average of once a week. And I was
in there with her every single time. I saw her body convulse from
the shock. Every single time.

One of these times that we'd ended up in the hospital, I just
wanted to lighten the mood a little bit, so I took her to a store across
the street. There was a basket of cards on the ground, and one of
the cards had these bright red roses gorgeously etched on them. She
saw them and she said, "Oh, Mommy, look how beautiful! I want
these to be my wedding invitations!"

So I bought them for her, and I went to a friend and had her
make three hundred identical cards. Because sometimes you need

to have the audacity to believe that it will all be okay, that it is okay to have the same kinds of dreams as everyone else.

Today, Laura is thirty-eight. When she was planning her wedding a few years ago, I went into my attic and pulled out that old box of invitations. I gave them to her one day, and I said, "You know you don't have to use them." I didn't want the memories associated with those years to be a stain on her special day. She said, "I know I don't have to, but I really want to." And so she did.

I'm a grandma now, to a set of twins. When the twins were born, the parents of that nurse who passed away from cancer sent us a gift—they had made the twins bracelets from one of the nurse's necklaces. It was a gentle reminder of what we'd all survived, a protective talisman for the little ones. And Laura is an exceptional mom, an amazing person. She hasn't let her limitations instill fear in her. She is a warrior woman, so brave, and I'm so proud of her. She takes my breath away.

Zarah, early twenties

I attended a top school in my country—a coed university that specializes in STEM education. There were only fifteen women in my class, in a sea of men. I was the first woman in my family to be allowed to pursue higher education. I had envisioned a very ambitious life for myself—a fulfilling career, some travel, and perhaps marriage and children later on. I abandoned hope when, a few months into college, my parents told me they'd started looking around for possible marriage proposals.

I should have seen this coming, but I guess I had thought that my parents would be different. My father and mother were supportive of me going to college, even though it was very expensive. I made ends meet by tutoring. I was very independent, and I was raised to stand up for myself and seek more from life. I had expected, at the very least, that I would be able to pick the person I'd marry.

My mother approached me one day and told me they'd found a nice match for me in the UK. I cringed. I frantically searched his name on Facebook and LinkedIn but found nothing except photos of fast cars and a sparsely populated work history. In a panic, I told them I knew nothing about him—that I couldn't be expected to marry just anyone. What about his education? In my experience, men who are more educated are less likely to be very religiously conservative. I feared that he might treat me like a piece of property for the rest of my life, not let me work, or not let me have my own thoughts.

"He'll be here in a week, for his sister's wedding," my mother told me. "And you'll have a chance to meet him, and then we can have your engagement ceremony."

The day came quickly. I spoke to him for a few minutes—there was no connection whatsoever, it seemed totally preposterous that I was supposed to share a life with this stranger—and I went back to my parents in tears. I told them, categorically, no. They sat me down over the next several weeks and, underhandedly, made it clear that I had no choice in the matter: "This is what we'll do for your wedding," my mother would say, showing me photos and brochures.

The more I tried to resist, the more they began to taunt me: "Do you think you're too good now—because you're educated? You're becoming arrogant." And when the coercion failed, they appealed to my reason: "You can't turn him down; it will cause a rift between our families. We'll be shamed in our community. If you don't care about us, at least think about your brother and sister."

The back-and-forth went on for six months. The more I resisted, the more they panicked until, one morning, my father came into my room while I was sleeping. He whisked the sheets off the bed and dragged me along my bedroom floor. He was taking me to a local religious figure so that he could pray for me. I started crying, his yelling ringing in my ears, sending chills down my spine. I'd never seen my father so angry before. I'd always viewed him as benevolent and incapable of violence, but the look in his eyes that day was foreign. When he hit me the first time, I was so shocked that I didn't quite register it. We both paused and looked at one another, acknowledging what had just happened. And then, as if that first smack had unleashed some pent-up anger in him, he kept going and going—hitting me while I cowered on the floor, hiding my face.

In between my fingers, I caught a glimpse of my mother. She was standing aside, looking down at me. I had hoped that she would intervene, that she would bring him back to his senses. I looked for pity in her eyes, for understanding or leniency. Or perhaps just for love, for a basic acknowledgment that seeing me like this pained her. But what I saw—her arms crossed, her eyes staring down at me, her nostrils flared—looked more like disgust.

I finally got away from him and locked myself in the bathroom.

He screamed and yelled for a few more minutes, pounding on the door, and then eventually the noise subsided. I stayed put for two hours until I heard a faint knock on the door.

"Zarah. You can come out now. They're gone." It was my sister.

"Swear it," I told her. "Swear that they're actually gone." I feared that they'd put her up to lying to me.

Thankfully, a few days later, I convinced a close family friend to look into this guy I was meant to marry. She had family in the UK, and word came back that he was barely employed and not the most reputable character.

"Don't pressure your daughter," she told my mother meaningfully.

When I came back home from a long day of classes, my parents sat me down and told me they'd decided to refuse his proposal.

I breathed easy for the first time in months, thinking the worst was behind me. But I was a few months shy of graduation when my parents came to me with another proposal—this one, from the US. I was distracted with finals and, having dodged one setup, felt strangely less threatened by this one, so the months went by quickly. Before I knew it, I was sitting across from him in my parents' living room and he was asking me about my plans after college. He told me he wanted his wife to be educated and to work, to have ambition. I guess he was trying to make sure that I wasn't trapping him into a marriage just so I could come to America. The next day, our parents announced our engagement. The next, we had the engagement ceremony; at the end of the week, he went back to the States.

My parents wanted the marriage ceremony to happen quickly— within the next three months. I was so depressed, and so in denial about what was happening, that I decided I would try to kill myself before we had a chance to marry. I started taking Panadol, the equivalent of Tylenol, after googling its cumulative effects. On any given day, I'd take anywhere from eight to twelve, hoping that, by the time my marriage arrived, it would have killed me. But it didn't—I threw up many times, lost a lot of weight, stopped getting my period, and I probably destroyed my liver, but I didn't die.

I was terribly depressed, with no way out. I looked to my parents to save me, but they had no mercy. My grandmother had an arranged marriage; my own mother had an arranged marriage. This is all they knew—and if it had been good enough for them, it would be good enough for me. Whenever I spoke out, my mother or father beat me. And my little sister looked on fearfully, catching a glimpse of what would likely be her own future.

After my future husband returned to the States, he added me on Facebook—which is how we communicated for the next couple of months. The conversation was dry. He didn't seem all too interested in me—never told me that he liked me or that he was looking forward to a life with me. But I guess I didn't say anything of the sort, either.

In January, one month before our big wedding celebration, I reached out to this guy I'd met in school, kind of like a last-ditch effort. I told him about the situation at home, and about the fact that I was, in the eyes of the law, spoken for. In my stupid daydreams, I had imagined him saying that he'd save me—that he would go to my parents and ask to marry me, instead. Of course, he did no such thing. He did something that I can only appreciate now. He encouraged me to speak up for myself: "If you don't speak up now, you're shutting up for the rest of your life."

"The worst thing that could happen," he said, with a wry smile on his face, "is that they could kill you." And with my life on the line, I called my fiancé and told him that I'd changed my mind, that I'd been pressured into the engagement. We hung up, and I shut myself in my room, waiting for the storm. No time at all went by. The phone rang and it was his mother—my future mother-in-law. I heard my mother's voice get more and more frantic as she spoke on the phone in the next room.

She pushed the door open, and in a flash, she was slapping me. "God will never forgive you," she kept saying. She made me call his mother and recant. At the time, I still had faith in Allah. I thought, *He won't let something happen to an innocent person*, so I kept praying for a miracle.

But the day of my wedding came. I was freaked out, and, judging by the look on my husband-to-be's face, so was he.

"You're not really getting married yet," my father told us. "This is just a formality. It's just a contract. It will be months before you're living together. You have time to decide."

My fiancé seemed mollified. I wasn't. I knew it was a lie. I was about to sign my life away.

In a haze—I don't remember much except that my heart seemed to be exploding—I signed the *nikah*. I was a married woman, just like that—forever bound to someone I'd spoken to in person once before, for less than a half hour. I was trapped. If you get divorced after you sign the *nikah*, you become a pariah, "a bad woman." People won't talk to you; they won't sit near you. You can't get married again. So women tolerate a lot of things—they tolerate abuse—because the alternative is worse. I've never known anyone to get divorced, no matter her situation.

The day after the wedding, my husband and I had breakfast together. There we were—married and barely speaking. He went back to the States and started the paperwork to bring me along. In the meantime, I had to go back to finish the last two months of college. I was so depressed, so absolutely hopeless, that I emailed the registrar and withdrew from all my classes. Once my parents got wind of it, though, the threats started again. They told me that if I didn't go back to finish, they wouldn't let my sister go to college. They weren't concerned about me, of course. They feared that my not being a college graduate would lower my "value" in the eyes of my husband.

I managed to finish out my degree only after speaking to a school therapist.

She told me, "You'll remember this moment in a few years' time. Don't let it be one that you regret."

My parents kept up their steady pressure: "Talk to your husband," they told me. "Create an understanding about the type of marriage you want."

In the meantime, they took me to the US embassy in our country to get our end of the immigration application finished. We started packing my things.

"We're going to miss you so much," they kept telling me, which rang untrue.

Once the application was approved, my husband came to pick me up and then we flew back together—a brutal flight, about twenty-four hours in all. And that's how I ended up here—in a big city, married to a complete stranger, living with his parents and his siblings. On the way over, I kept thinking, *If it's not tolerable, if he beats me, I will leave him, or I will kill myself,* to set my heart at ease.

But he's a really wonderful person. He's not conservative—with his encouragement, I've started taking classes. I'm not enrolled in a degree program, but the hope is that someday my résumé will be sharp enough to apply for a master's program in engineering. My husband tells me that he wants to see me be interested in life; he wants me to be happy. His parents are amazing. His father cooks for us—"You're both my children," he says—and his mom, who is an entrepreneur, encourages me to stand up to her son: "Fight with him when you disagree; don't just say yes."

But when my parents call, my heart won't allow me to talk to them. They didn't see what it was like here for the first few months—how lonely I was, how much I wished for death. They will see the situation now—80 percent luck, and 20 percent determination to survive—and take credit for it. My father will say, "You see? I arranged marriages for six of my siblings, and I was never wrong." I am happy with my husband—as happy as I can be with someone I didn't know when I married him—but I'm not ready to thank my parents for that. How can I? I could have very well ended up with the guy in London—the one who couldn't even hold down a job.

I met with my friends from college the other week—they're both single, independent, and attending graduate schools in the States. I can't help but envy them. I could have been in their position. I try not to live in the past; what happened, happened. But I fear for other women who don't fare as well as I have. My heart aches for them. My heart aches for my little sister.

Andy, early forties

Exactly thirty-eight minutes of my day are mine. I wake up every morning at five o'clock and get myself ready for work. I brush my teeth, shower, and groom—in that order. Then, I look over my work emails while I'm walking downstairs to the kitchen, where my wife is waiting with a cup of already-brewed coffee.

I tell her good morning, usually without looking up from my phone. I grab the coffee in one hand and gulp it down in one go, setting it back down on the marble counter with a clink that signals I'm ready for my second cup. Then I grab an apple and head back upstairs to wake up the kids. It's five forty-five.

By six thirty, the kids are dressed and their lunches are packed. I've asked them if they've done their homework, and they've nodded with a roll of their eyes—an obligatory gesture at their age. I make a mental note to engage them more, to find out more about their lives, but there's not enough time. There's never enough time.

In the next ten minutes, I give my wife a kiss—our only form of intimacy in the last several months—and I head to my car. She will drop off the kids before driving to work herself. My thoughts for the next nineteen minutes will be occupied by myriad worries.

I arrive at work at roughly 7:00 a.m. I greet my coworkers and grab yet another cup of coffee on my way to my office. And then I work, often uninterrupted, until late afternoon. I work hard because I'm in my early forties and these are peak years for upward mobility. But that's the short answer.

The long answer is that I lose myself in work to avoid feeling like I'm being gulped up by an unexciting, unremarkable life. One of my biggest sources of anxiety is that my wife and I haven't had sex in over six months. We've been married for eighteen years, and in those years—well, especially in the last five years—the space be-tween us seems to keep growing. Any attempt I make at breaching the gap seems contrived; she thinks that it's all a means to an end, the end being sex. But honestly, I want to feel that we're not just roommates—that we're not just waiting for the kids to grow up so that we can move on. It's starting to become very apparent that maybe we've just changed, that maybe things are becoming irrecon-cilable.

But it's not all her fault. We have separate bedtimes, and she often stays up to study or catch up on work. I do, too. There have been times when she's tried to initiate intimacy and I've turned her down. I tell her that I'll be up in a minute, but then I get caught up with work, or I decide I need a shower. I realize I'm making excuses. And that worries me.

We both work in the same field, and it's a highly competitive one. I have a higher position, but she recently chose to go back to school and finish her MBA so that she can have access to better op-portunities. She left her job and got a better position in manage-ment, so I think she feels that it was worth the sacrifice. My goal this year was to move up the ladder, to get a raise—and I did, so I feel better about my station, too. I supported my wife's goal, but she says that I secretly begrudge her success. In a lot of ways, it does seem like a zero-sum game. We don't directly compete, but you can see how our respective goals lead to each making demands of the other's time. Any time that she spent with her schoolwork is time that I had to spend compensating—whether it's for housework or parenting chores.

It doesn't help that we have entirely different parenting styles. She's strict, and I'm more laid-back; the kids see this and, being kids, they pit us against each other. I let them get away with it, which upsets her endlessly. For example, it's the fourteen-year-old's responsibility to do the dishes after dinner every night. She reminds him, and he says (usually while engrossed in a TV show or video game), "I'll get to it in a few minutes." She gets aggravated, then firm, then she starts to nag. If that doesn't work, she escalates the situation: "You better do it now, or I will take away the TV." So then he appeals to me, and I take his side because he's just a kid, and he doesn't need to be so serious about everything just yet. I tell her to relax, to let him do it on his own time as long as it gets done. She tells me that I'm teaching my kids to procrastinate. And then the night is shot.

I spend money on them—on us—money that she doesn't think we have. I love taking the boys to baseball games, and I spend about $500 a game—seats, food, and transportation. That's good family-bonding time and good entertainment. But she thinks that it's too much money and the kids will feel entitled. She has a very firm grip on our finances, and we always fight about it. She has access to my bank account—what I make and what I spend, and she'll often micromanage it. I bought some tools for a home-improvement project, and she wanted me to return them. I refused. It seems like we fight about everything lately because she assumes that I'll contradict her for the sake of contradicting. It's getting rough; being in this marriage is burning up so much energy that it feels like I'm holding down a second job.

My growing detachment must have been pretty obvious because a few months ago, she looked through my phone and found texts from a woman I'd met on Craigslist. We had been corresponding regularly and having an emotional affair—I reached out to her for support, I guess. Marie was also married and had issues with her husband. Misery loves company, and you get to a place where you convince yourself that it's part of marriage. It's crap, and everyone is suffering. Even when people are holding hands and smiling, they're miserable in their homes. You become very cynical about what marriage is.

"This is not what normal people do," my wife told me. "And if that's what you want to do, then you're on your own."

So it was an ultimatum of sorts. I needed to step up. I realized that we were trying to do too much. We were trying to have it all, and we got burnt out. We were like tinder—it only took one little spark to fire us up. My wife offered to put her MBA on hold to give us a fighting chance, but I had promised to support her, and I wanted to deliver. So things just got worse.

Eventually my wife said, "If you want to be serious about us getting better, we need counseling—individually, but you probably need it more."

I told her that I felt anxious about so many things, and she said she felt it, too, but she had chosen not to take it out on our relationship.

What struck me most was her suggestion that perhaps I was someone who wanted to exist in the context of a family but, when it all came down to it, I wanted to do my own thing. She told me that I needed to figure out what I wanted before we could move forward.

She said, basically: "Even if you go to therapy and proclaim that you're in a better place, what's to stop you from going back to [emotionally cheating] once the spotlight is off of you?"

At first, I thought, *Wow, she's throwing a lot on me.* But then I figured, *Okay, I'll do it. I'll commit to therapy. We'll see what happens.* So now I have a standing therapy session on Fridays from 8:30 to 9:30 a.m. This therapist provides me with tools to confront my issues without getting flustered and hopeless. It's like religion. It only works if you believe in it and go through the rituals of it. I think that the practice of setting aside the time for my feelings opened up a little bit of my blocked emotions. I also realized that my wife saw I was putting in the time "to go to church" and making an effort. So it was a positive thing for us.

It has helped me learn that love evolves over time. The romance and the emotional part become secondary. The practicalities of life—the obligations and responsibilities, the loop jumping—they take precedence. We're in a better place now. With therapy, we've been able to get over the chasm that was opened between us. We're not 100 percent back to where it was twenty years ago when we first met, but we have to have everything else working properly in order for us to get to the point of having intimate, satisfying sex. Right now, we're getting our needs met. It's not raging hormones and amazing, mind-blowing sex—we're just working on repairing our relationship. So we keep jumping through the hoops, sticking to our routine.

Around 6:00 p.m. every day, I usually get a text from my wife. *Where are you?* she wants to know. Sometimes, *Are you avoiding us?* Maybe I still am. I reluctantly get back in my car and for another nineteen minutes, I am on my own. There are no children demanding to watch just five more minutes of their TV show. There is no wife nagging me about money, or about working too much or not working hard enough. It is quiet and I get to visit with my thoughts, and for a little while, I feel all right.

As I pull up to the third stop sign from my house, though, anxiety bubbles in the pit of my stomach and I slow the car down to a crawl. I keep going, little by little, meaning to stop any second now—but the driveway slips away, and then I can see it in the rearview mirror. I drive around the block once more, twice more, and then I finally park.

Federico, twenties

I was ten years old when we moved to the States from South America. We lived a comfortable life there—we were middle-class, and my parents owned several shoe stores. But we were drawn to the DC area by the classic immigrant dream: safety, a better life. My mom and dad came with me, and we left my younger siblings with my aunt back home. The plan was that we would try to bring them here once we got things in order. Or to make a little bit of money and go back. Eight years passed in a heartbeat.

We left my siblings behind when they were seven and eight, respectively. The next time my mother saw them, they were teenagers. My aunt passed away from cancer, and my mom had to go back home. She's there now, taking care of my siblings and my aunt's children, too. I haven't seen her in three years. This has torn our family apart, and the only solace I feel is in knowing that it's for a greater good. I can't imagine what it must be like for my father, not to see his wife and children. I can't imagine what it must be like for my mother, to be away from me. We speak on the phone and see each other on video every day, but it is not the same. During almost every call, someone brings up how our sacrifice "will all be worth it," usually when talking about my education. And when we say goodbye, my mother always cries. Every time I talk to her, I think, *Maybe today she won't cry.*

I played soccer in high school, and I was very good. I had opportunities to play overseas, but I couldn't pursue them because I'm not a citizen. I was not driven when I was younger. All I wanted to do was play soccer professionally and I couldn't do that, so I gave it up. We came here legally, with a visa that we overstayed, so now we have no road to citizenship. There aren't very many job opportunities for undocumented kids with no path to citizenship, so my dad told me that I had to work construction with him. I started when I was eighteen, right after I graduated high school. I was a kid. Working with my dad put a lot of stress on our relationship. I was afraid often—I felt totally unqualified. We were building something with our hands, and the responsibility of what we were doing was heavy. What if someone got hurt because of a mistake I made? Everything felt big, and it made me feel very small.

But all that doubt and fear went away when I got my first paycheck. I felt rich. I saved my money and sent it back to my family. When my mother moved back, my father, uncle, and I all moved in together in a studio apartment. Shortly thereafter, my dad and I both got laid off. It's not like you have job security when you're undocumented; one day you have a job, the next you don't, and that's just the way it is. Who are you going to complain to? Who is going to care? I remember how horrible those months were. My uncle was working in events and planning for a university, so he would bring us leftover food from their events. Whole months went by of eating leftover sandwiches with little toothpicks in them. That's how we survived.

When we found work again, it taught me the value of money. For my dad, it was a bittersweet experience. When school and my dreams of playing professional soccer didn't pan out for me, I think he thought it was fine for his eldest to do some manual labor, to learn what it meant to go to sleep dog-tired at the end of the day. But he saw the stress that work, and then unemployment, put on me, and I think he realized that maybe I was still too young to be learning these lessons. I noticed that he was working hard—much harder than before—and he would often cover my work, too. He said that it hurt him to see me doing such hard physical labor. He felt bad for me, and I understand. I would want a better life for my son, too.

He had an accident at work one day: he fell off an eight-foot ladder. He was unconscious on the floor, and I called the ambulance in a panic. When we got to the hospital, I could tell that he was in a lot of pain, but the doctors kept telling us that he was fine. We didn't have insurance, so they didn't want to treat him. We eventually just went home. My dad never went back to work—he couldn't. His back has never been the same; he has trouble getting up from a seated position, and when he straightens out his body, his face goes red from the pain. At around the time of my father's injury, the university my uncle worked for found out that he didn't have papers, and they fired him. So we gave my uncle my father's tools, and he started working construction with me.

After that, I started downloading books online about becoming a foreman and a project manager. I paid attention at work and asked my boss questions when I didn't understand why we were doing something; I took ownership of my work, and my boss slowly started giving me more and more responsibility. After a couple of years, he gave me opportunities to manage jobs on my own. But that didn't change the fact that I still didn't have a work permit. It didn't matter how hard I tried or how good I was at my job, because at the end of the day I was still undocumented, with no solution in sight.

I don't remember how I met her, but I should have seen it coming. A couple of months into us knowing each other, she said that she saw how difficult it was for me to be away from my family and that she would marry me so that I could get my papers. I told her that I wasn't sure I wanted to be married right now—I had feelings for her, but I'd only known her for a little while, and I definitely wasn't sure that she was someone I wanted to marry. I had a lot of doubts about it, but she said she understood that it was a marriage of convenience. It seemed too good to be true, but I went along with it because I thought it would be a quick fix to so many of my problems.

We went to city hall, and shortly after we got married, I got a conditional green card, which meant that I'd have to be with her for another two years if I wanted to get citizenship. They do this so that people don't take advantage of the process and then get divorced as soon as they get their papers. But almost immediately, she started getting very jealous and possessive. She told me that she felt I would eventually fall in love with her. I was completely dependent on her and her whims—she threatened to divorce me or tell the government that it was a sham marriage—and I guess she knew she had me where she wanted me. Eventually, all these small financial emergencies started coming up: a fix for the car here, new furniture there. She and her mother were constantly hitting me up for money.

By the time I asked her for a divorce, about a year in, I was totally broke and an anxious wreck. But I had decided that my health and peace of mind came before a stupid piece of paper. She, of course, completely refused to grant me the divorce. I couldn't take it anymore, so I showed up at the immigration office and told them everything. They said they'd cancel my application, and a lot of money, heartache, and anxiety later, I was right back where I started. The whole experience was really traumatic for me and my family. We are not the types of people who cause trouble and break rules. We are not criminals. I did this because I had no other option, and I really scared myself and my parents when it didn't work out.

But things did look up for me. A year or two after the divorce, I met Ana. Her story is as crazy as mine. She was born in Latvia to alcoholic parents. Unable to care for their children, they passed the three daughters on to their grandmother. When she passed away, the older daughters ended up on the streets. Ana was lucky enough to be put into a Latvian orphanage that had connections with the States. While she was under their care, she went from foster parent to foster parent for years. When she turned thirteen, she was told that a sixty-one-year-old former nurse from America wanted to adopt her. She came here on a trial basis and loved it—loved her new mom, too. So she stayed. And, eventually, she met me. She always tells me, "You don't have to be blood to be family." We're getting married next year.

I feel like I never had a childhood. I had so many people—my mom, my siblings, my aunt's kids—depending on me from such a young age. I work all the time—we all do—so that we can support each other. I don't waste money on luxuries, I don't drink, and I don't do drugs. I don't get in trouble with the law. I just keep my head down and work so that my family and my siblings can have a better life, a better future. The sacrifice we have made as a family, to break in two so that we can have better lives, is not something I take lightly. But also, what does that mean—better lives? It's hard to quantify. Is not seeing my mother worth a better paycheck? When my aunt died, it brought things into perspective. My mother could die, and I would not be able to go to her funeral.

I'm not sure there's a happy ending for all of us as a family—if my father wants to see his wife and children again, he will have to go back to South America, which means leaving me here. My mother and my siblings won't be able to come to my wedding, which makes me very sad. I have to believe that all our sacrifices will count for something—that my life in this country matters, that maybe my children will be able to chase their dreams because of their father. Who knows? Maybe one of them will be a soccer star. I have to believe it. Otherwise, it would be impossible to wake up every morning.

Gemma, early twenties

I met my boyfriend in college. I was out to lunch with a girlfriend of mine and we were at a cafeteria-style spot on campus. He and a friend of his sat down next to us, and I remember immediately feeling that they were kind of looking at us and talking about us. We were both single at the time, so we reciprocated—we were having the type of conversations that you have when you know people are overhearing.

I remember I'd gotten Thai noodles from the buffet bar and the peanut sauce kept spraying all over my face. I'd forgotten to get napkins, and my friend said loudly, "You look ridiculous. You need a bib."

And he kind of leaned over (he was a table away from us), and he said, "For what it's worth, I think you look adorable. But here's your bib." And he gave me a napkin.

This is far from a great romance, but I was nineteen, and I thought he was cute—cute enough to go out on a couple of dates, maybe. Before we left for class, we exchanged numbers with both of them. I remember not being super excited about him; I didn't have butterflies or anything, which is really interesting because every single guy I've dated seriously since, I've had immediate "butterflies" for. He's the only guy I've ever dated to whom I wasn't super physically attracted.

So anyways, I was studying at the library the next day when he texted me and asked if I was doing anything. I blew off my work and went to hang out with him, and the rest is history. I should also mention that he was quite a bit older than me—by almost a decade—he'd taken time off after college and was actually in the graduate school there.

I was supposed to be living in the dorms at school. He lived off campus, and we were spending so much time together that I ended up basically moving in with him. It all happened in the span of a month—we met, started hanging out, and then most of my stuff was at his place. My roommate at the time (whom I met maybe three times), was this Russian girl who was super thin and beautiful and aloof, and I remember "moving in" my things to the room we were supposed to share and then gradually moving everything back out to his spot. I basically had maybe three pieces of clothing there and a pair of shoes. Everything else was over at his apartment.

I was relatively inexperienced sexually, so I wanted to kind of take things slowly. I had slept with two guys before him, and I really didn't want to "catch feelings" even though we were moving quickly. So I remember the first time we slept together, I was thinking— *We're just fucking. This isn't serious. You can walk away.* We were in bed afterward, talking and hanging out, and he turned to me and told me he loved me. I just laughed out loud. I thought it was so ridiculous that this man—this *older* man—was telling me he was in love with me after we'd just had sex for the first time. But he seemed upset by the fact that I was laughing, and I thought to myself, *Oh, maybe he's serious. Maybe he really does love me.*

Which is fucking ridiculous. Because we'd just met.

But things got progressively more intense. At first, I liked that he was older. He just seemed more real. I was still worrying about college and credits, and he had a job and was going to school for a career. He smoked. He drank things like Scotch. He'd had jobs before. He'd had serious girlfriends. He was a real person, and that he was interested in me made me feel like I was also more interesting, more of an adult.

I met his parents, who absolutely hated me because I was "too young" and we didn't have anything in common. He met my parents, who absolutely hated him because he was "too old" and we didn't have anything in common. And although we fought about our parents not accepting us as a couple, things were fine, for the most part.

But slowly, over maybe the span of a year, I started noticing that his life was taking over my life. I wasn't paying attention to school. I wasn't hanging out with my friends. I wasn't doing any of the things that used to make me happy, like working out or going out to party. I was basically not in college anymore. We hung out with his friends, and whenever I'd want him to hang out with mine, he'd very nicely and diplomatically decline, or tell me he had work, or tell me school was really busy. I liked his friends fine, but I always felt like an idiot around them. They were all older and super dismissive of me. I was basically seen as the hot chick their friend was fucking around with for a little while.

So I became increasingly isolated. We started fighting a lot, and I was drinking more, too. I'd never been a drinker—it was actually still illegal for me to drink when we met—so he really initiated me into the world of having a drink at the end of the day. And over time it became a habit. I'd drink to celebrate a good day. Drink to self-medicate after a bad day. Drink to end a day.

I remember we'd had a bad fight and I was drunk on red wine. I went into the shower to sober myself up and this song came on, on Spotify, about missing an old love. And I started thinking about Matt, my first boyfriend in college. He'd graduated a year before me and moved back home. Even though we loved each other and things were good, being long-distance was difficult. We had decided to very amicably break up, trusting that life would bring us together again if it was meant to be.

The more I thought about Matt, the more it kind of tempered the sadness that I felt over my boyfriend. It was almost like my brain was looking at Matt as someone who would always be there, maybe as the guy I was meant to be with all along. So I texted him. Things were kind of awkward in our first few messages because he knew from my social media that I was with someone else and I'd seen that he was dating someone, too. But we hit our stride again and made plans for me to visit him the next day.

My boyfriend and I weren't talking, and I just told him I was going to go visit a friend. I packed some clothes and took the train to Matt. He picked me up from the station, and seeing him was really good; it felt right. I gave him a hug, but we didn't kiss. We went back to his place, and it was a little awkward because we didn't really want to acknowledge that we both had significant others, but it was obvious that we were both pushing the line of what was appropriate.

We slept in the same bed and cuddled, but there was a distance between us. On my end, I guess it was because I was still hoping to work things out with my boyfriend. We talked about Matt's current girlfriend, too. Things didn't seem super serious, but I felt guilty about what we were doing. I remember I was in Matt's bathroom while he was at work and I was looking through his medicine cabinet for his cologne. He used to wear Aventus by Creed, and I would always steal some from him when we were together. I sprayed some on, and it just brought all our memories back to me. I decided I'd try to get back together with him. I was pretty sure of where he stood, too. I knew we still had strong feelings for each other.

While I waited for Matt to get home from work, my boyfriend called. I hadn't heard from him during the time I'd been away, so I answered. And he said something like, "Okay, this is enough now. You've made your point. Please come back home." So I took the first train back. I didn't even tell Matt I was leaving.

My boyfriend never asked where I'd been. I think he just didn't want to know, but he had a sense. Things between us were fine for a while, but then we'd fight again. Every time we fought, I'd try to give myself an out—I'd go out on a date with some guy from school, or distract myself with old flames. I always flirted, but I never crossed the line. And I noticed that he was keeping his distance, too. He seemed cagey and distracted. He never left his phone unattended. He password-protected his computer. He'd come home late from work and make up all these excuses. I never suspected that he was cheating because I'd never dealt with infidelity before. I just didn't think someone would cheat on *me*, although I'd obviously emotionally cheated on him.

We went back and forth in this awful pattern of fighting, breaking up, making up, having sex, fighting again, and repeat. But eventually we stopped having sex, and although I wanted to and kept
asking him what was wrong, he just claimed he was tired. I was so
stupid and naive that I totally bought it and was trying to be an understanding girlfriend.

———————

We'd been together for about three years when this girl he worked
with called me and told me that they'd been sleeping together for
two years. I actually knew her really well, and she had become a
friend of mine. We routinely invited her over to dinner parties and
hung out with her probably every week. I actually *liked* her, which
made it worse. Apparently she had gotten fed up with him lying to
both of us and decided to come clean. She also told me a lot of other
things that I didn't know about him—mainly, that he'd been married
before. The divorce went through right before he and I met. So I
had a friend help me hack into his computer, and I basically saw all
the photos he'd saved of the wedding with this other girl, along with
some pretty graphic photos of them together. It made me feel really
sick to my stomach.

The breakup had been coming for a while, but I never thought
that's what would do it. Now, looking back on it, I feel really manip-
ulated. He was older, and he knew what he was doing. He took advantage of my innocence and basically wasted my time. I spent
three years being this idiot's arm candy. I wish I'd slept with Matt
when I had the chance.

The breakup was clean, though. I found my own apartment and
moved out, in a week's time. I got myself on a few dating apps and
got back into the swing of things. I texted this guy I'd flirted with in
college, visited him in New York, and we had sex on his rooftop,
overlooking downtown Manhattan. I always loved that saying: *The
best way to get over someone is to get under someone.*

Sam, thirty-seven

I've been divorced and single for a few years now. I've been dating people on and off, but you could say I'm stuck in the daily routine of life—I go to work, I hang out with friends, or I work out. For the most part, I'm happy. Every once in a while, though, when I'm driving home from work and I go over the bridge that used to take me to the home my ex-wife and I made together, or when a certain song comes on, I'm reminded of her. I get overcome by this awful feeling of missing her. It's not sexual—definitely not—it's more similar to how I miss my kids, except not quite as bad. You know that feeling, after you've spent all day at work and you come home to a houseful of kids? My kids used to jump on me, literally climb me, and whatever had been weighing on my heart would just melt off, gone. I used to look forward to that moment all day. And that's kind of how I feel about my ex. I miss that feeling of happiness I'd get when she hugged me at the end of a long day. My ex-wife feels a lot of anger toward me and the choices I made, though. So I very much doubt she ever misses me.

I was twenty-three when I met my now ex. It was on Yahoo! Personals. I came across her profile, and it was really nicely written. She'd said that she was new in town and wanted to meet people. Back in the day, to message someone you liked you had to pay something like $30. So I bit the bullet and messaged her. But I never heard back. I wrote her again—something cheesy about myself and what I liked in her profile—and in the course of the message, I told her that I'd been an extra in a movie. And it happened to be one of her favorite movies. We went to Starbucks on our first date, and we bought candy afterward and ate it out of the bag. Our second date was at an Italian restaurant. And we were kind of inseparable after that. I spent all my free time with her.

I was twenty-five when I married her, and twenty-seven when we had our first kid. Looking back, I realize that I hardly had the mental capacity to make big life decisions then—and yet we did. At first, I would say things were going well. We did a lot of silly but important things together, like we'd watch movies or TV shows that we both loved, we'd bond over music, or we'd cook together. These little things that we spent time on were what made our marriage really special. We had sex probably twice a week at that point. But then twice a week turned into twice a month, and even less. And then, at one point, after we had our first kid, it completely stopped. We went without sex for two years.

Eventually, she decided to get pregnant again and the sex started again. Once we conceived, it stopped for another two years, and it went on like this—sex only to conceive and nothing beyond that—for the rest of our marriage. For me, the loneliness and depression got so bad that I would silently cry myself to sleep every night. The feeling was like a sheet of ice-cold air under the uppermost layer of my skin—like someone had taken one of those fireplace bellows and driven the cold through my toes, all the way up to my head. And in my misery, I'd imagine her reaching over and touching my shoulder to comfort me, and I often think, now, how different things might have been had she ever done that. But she never did.

So, my options at that point were to either cheat or get a divorce, and I didn't want to leave my family, so I decided to cheat. It was with someone who was in town on business; I found her online. She was also in a sexless relationship. We spoke for a few hours in person, and the next day I drove to her hotel to have sex with her. That drive was terrifying. My father was a cheater, and I never wanted to be like him. But when it was done, I didn't feel bad. It was more *The Bridges of Madison County* than a cheap tabloid. It felt like the people who were vowed to us wouldn't help us with our pain, so we had to rely on strangers. Since that drive to the hotel, nothing scares me. I'm not afraid like I used to be.

Over the course of the next two years, I cheated on my ex-wife with nineteen people. She found out because I broke my "rules" for someone. The rules were just general guidelines I followed so that I wouldn't allow myself to get too close. The most important was not to sleep with the same person more than a couple of times. The idea was that I didn't want to develop feelings for someone else. But I made an exception, and I let things get too far. When I tried to call things off with her, she went all *Fatal Attraction* on me. After she threatened to tell my boss about the affair and have me killed, she emailed my wife and told her everything.

We tried therapy. She went to one therapy session with me, and I continued going alone for quite a while; I guess she thought this was my problem to deal with and she was blameless. She moved back to her home state temporarily—she needed some distance and to be close to her family, which is a huge source of support and stability for her. She and the kids were a plane ride away, and I visited them whenever work allowed. I decided to stop cheating and to focus on fixing our marriage. Things went back to somewhat normal for a few months, and she moved back. She got pregnant a third time, and after we had the baby, the sex stopped again. Now, three kids and a mortgage, I get it—sex is not a priority. We were tired, we were stressed out, and most nights at least one kid was sleeping in bed with us. But it wasn't just the sex that I missed, it was the intimacy. I'd come home from work and go to give her a hug, and she'd put her hands on my chest and push me off. I'd try to snuggle her at night, and she'd kick me off and complain she was hot. If you've never had someone you love so much you'd die for her do that to you, well, let me tell you, it's the worst fucking feeling in the world.

Eight months into that, I met a woman who was a swinger. We knew each other from work, and we trusted each other because we both had something to lose. And more importantly, there was mutual attraction. It seemed like a safe way to meet my needs without getting emotionally involved. Unfortunately, I made the mistake of leaving my iPad at home for my son to play with one day, while I was at work. During the course of the day, I was texting with this woman about where to meet, and all the texts were also going to the iPad. So I got a call at work from my wife. She was screaming. She said, "If you're not home in the next twenty minutes, I'm leaving, and I'm taking the kids." And that was it—the end.

She had told me the first time around that if she ever caught me cheating again, it would be over. I went home that day, and she said she wanted a divorce. I'm not one to play games with people, so I agreed to it immediately. Later on, she asked to move back to her home state with our kids, and I let her do that, too, although it's far enough that I have to take several days off work to visit them—no quick weekend trips. Sometimes, I regret it. My kids are so far away now. I see them as often as I can, but my ex is engaged to this guy who is so racist and just—has totally different values—and I'm so afraid that my kids will pick that up. Although, they're sharp as hell, so something tells me they'll know better than to listen to him.

To be honest, more often than not during our relationship, I felt like she was trying to sabotage our marriage by completely icing me out. I did something bad, yes—I self-medicated; I found other people who were hurting, and we provided each other adult company. I didn't cheat because I had some inherent drive to cheat; I did it because I was in pain and I desperately needed affection and human contact. I realize how pathetic that sounds, and I really don't miss how miserable I was back then. We had an unhappy marriage, although I'm sure that outwardly we seemed picture-perfect.

Thinking back on it now, I very clearly remember her telling me at some point during the course of our relationship, "If you ever cheat on me—that's it, it's over." And even so, she gave me a second chance. So maybe I was doing a bit of sabotaging myself. And when I really allow myself a moment of honesty, I know that we didn't have very much in common intellectually. She was religious; I'm not. She was conservative—at least, her family was. My family and I are not. So there wasn't much keeping us together besides weather talk and the customs that we'd created in our family. The kids were our only strong common bond.

Equally as hard as the divorce was telling my mom and family about what had happened. As I mentioned, my dad was a cheater. My mom's face, my siblings' faces, when I told them what I'd done—it was like the ultimate betrayal. They couldn't believe I was telling them the truth. And I get it. Honestly? Nineteen times? Even I think it's hard to justify that with "I was really sad" and "I missed intimacy." I'm shocked at myself, too. Something was broken, and I'm not sure it was ever fixable. Maybe her inability to be intimate with me and my cheating were a side effect of that brokenness.

But every once in a while, I miss her as a person. I miss eating ice cream with her and watching some nerdy show. I miss hiking with her or singing along to songs with her in the car. I really miss the home we built together. Every once in a while, when the weather is idyllic, I'll think, *God, it would be so nice to be at home, grilling in the backyard with my family*. I miss being parents to our kids with her—we were different, yeah, but we really clicked where it mattered: on values, morals, and how we treated people. And during these moments, I regret that I said yes to the divorce so quickly. Maybe if I'd waited for the cool-down period, things would be different. I don't know. I go back and forth.

I've never told her how I feel. Divorce is hard, and there are times when I feel like I got a really raw deal. I get the kids for eight weeks during the summer, and then I see them every other month for a few days. I don't think I'll ever get used to not seeing their faces every single day, like before. The pain of losing my family is like a phantom limb—my mind is trapped in the past, in what was. But I just have to believe that we made the right choice, and I have to move on.

Kurt, fifties

When I was a young kid, I imagined that God had an assembly line up in heaven where he and the angels put together new people. There would be arms and legs and toes and ears, and everything would go off without a hitch . . . for the most part. But every once in a while, there'd be an earthquake, and all the parts on the assembly line would be tossed around and jumbled, and someone would end up with an extra part or the wrong parts altogether. That's how my young mind used to reconcile it—that feeling that I couldn't quite understand, that something about my body was wrong—long before I learned to accept and love myself, long before I learned there is nothing wrong with me.

When I was in eighth grade, my sister started dating this guy and I couldn't understand why she was dating a boy, because I liked girls. In tenth grade, I wrote a love letter to one of my friends. It was very poetic; I saw myself in a different role, as a male courting someone. I tried to explain to her that even though I looked like a girl, I was actually a boy. I told her that I loved her. I think she was curious and flattered at first, but eventually I got called down to the school counselor's office during English class. My parents were there; hers were, too. My adviser told me to stop writing letters, and I remember that—at some point in the conversation—somebody used the word *lesbian*. I didn't feel lesbian.

For the longest time, I knew who I was, but other people did not. Despite what they said, I felt like a boy who liked girls. I'd spent the previous three years of my life asking my mother when I'd become a boy. I was holding out hope even after I got my period. I took care of that part of my anatomy, but I didn't identify with it psychologically. I was in my early twenties when I realized that this would be "it" for the rest of my life.

Really, who I was became a problem for me only because it was a problem for others. I was very active in the church and wanted to be a minister, but I knew that the church didn't accept "my kind," so I ended up leaving. In the meantime, I decided to camouflage myself as best as I could until I was able to get out of my small town. I knew that I needed to move somewhere far away from my family and everyone who had ever known me as a woman. I got a job and, with $400 in my bank account and a car that was perpetually breaking down, I moved to a different state—a bigger city. I slowly started building a group of friends who were like me—other trans people—and eventually I started feeling comfortable and safe enough to start transitioning.

I was forty years old when I began to transition. I think, subconsciously, I was waiting for my mother to die. She was very religious, and my transition would have killed her. It would have shamed her in her community, or it would have made her question her faith. I couldn't do that to her. So I waited. I went to counseling for a little over a year, which is required before one starts the process, and then I started using a testosterone patch. After eight months on the patch, I started giving myself testosterone injections, which I'll have to keep taking for the rest of my life. I wore a fake mustache every time I went out, mostly because picking bathrooms was becoming a problem.

My first surgery was a double mastectomy. Up until the surgery, I had been wrapping my breasts with ACE bandages, which was not only a hassle to do every single day but was also becoming pretty painful.

I can't describe to you how free I felt after that surgery. There's this paranoia that you carry around with you as you're transitioning that someone will figure out that you're not who you claim to be. I had nightmares that I would be somehow "discovered" as an impostor. After the surgery, I had moments during my day when I'd be going about things at work and then—all of a sudden—I'd feel this sense of relief and peace wash over me, and I'd start crying. Hope kept me going. I hoped that where I was headed was better than where I was. I hoped to feel better. Hope gave me courage. It gave me courage to suffer, even with no end in sight.

My second surgery was a total abdominal hysterectomy. I had my ovaries and my uterus removed. I had been disassociated from the anatomically female parts of my body for such a long time that I felt no emotional reaction to the surgery. However, the lack of estrogen sent me into menopause. At the end of the injection cycle, when the testosterone levels were also at their lowest, I would get hot flashes and night sweats. During the most trying periods of my life, I have found that my sense of humor keeps me afloat. Objectively, I found the fact that I was having hot flashes hilarious.

The last surgery I had was a metoidioplasty, in which the doctors cut the suspensory ligaments that hold the clitoris intact, and from the skin and surrounding area, they make a penis. Then they can put testicles in the labia majora. I was in pain for months afterward, but when it was done, I felt like myself for the first time in my life. I finally felt that I belonged. Imagine that—I was forty-five and experiencing my true self for the first time. I felt like a teenager all over again. Except I was a teenager with male-pattern baldness, because I lost some hair on the crown and back of my head.

The first person I dated as a man was my wife. I met her a few months after my full transition, and I explained my story on our fourth date. She said she needed to think about all of it, and then I didn't hear from her for a few days. I understood her hesitation, but my heart was in such pain. I kept thinking that rejection, after everything I'd gone through, would be the final nail in my coffin. But then she called me, and all she said was: "Eh, what the hell, let's give it a shot."

Give it a shot, we did. We worked around our sexual issues, and there were a few: namely, my size was not adequate for penetration. I could have gotten a different procedure, a phalloplasty, which would have been a better procedure for penetrative sex. It involves getting a piece of your own skin transplanted to form the penis and a balloon inserted to help you get "happy," but it has a higher complication rate.

She was a very patient and giving person. We ended up getting married. I loved her so damn much. I loved her in a way that was so new to me: I so hated for us to be apart that even our time together was painful, because I'd torture myself with the inevitability of having to part ways. So I could never quite enjoy her, because the joy was tinged by the thought of having to leave her to go to work. It's almost like the universe sensed my fear: we'd been married for six years when she was diagnosed with breast cancer. We fought it for three years. It took me a year after she had died to stop fighting—cancer, death, loss, the world—to realize she wasn't there anymore. I lost my best friend, my wife, and the only person who ever really knew me.

After she died, I isolated myself. I shut down and I felt so alone. Part of me never wanted to try again, to find another connection. Part of me was desperate for it. I wanted it all to have been easier. I wanted it to not have been such a fight. I wanted to be loved. I want to be understood. I want so many things, and, especially right after she died, I felt like I had nothing. I went to a bar one night, blind with rage, and I got blackout drunk. I went home with a guy, and I tried to have sex with him. He had to drive me to the ER because I nearly bled to death. I was desperate, though. I was desperate to feel "normal" and loved.

Some days, I still wake up angry. Those are wasted days, and there are still far too many of them. Now I have to start all over again, and it feels so late. How do I explain to a stranger who I am? How do I even start bridging that chasm? My identity makes my partners question their own sexuality. If they're attracted to someone who is male but used to be female—what does that make them?

Right after I lost my wife, I contemplated suicide. I thought of jumping off a bridge. But my sense of humor and my relationship with God kept me going. The church might have turned its back on me, but I have my own set of beliefs. God is my buddy, and God saw me through it. Plus, I had an uncle who committed suicide. That wasn't an option for me—it's the only decision you can't change. You can't change death.

I can't get my wife back, and I can't help but feel as though I've been ripped off. Not by a person, and not by God. Just by circumstance. I would like to be with someone who is okay with me, how I am, but it feels like it's too late, now. Women my age are used to men who are genetically male, and they're used to sex as they know it. Nothing else. And I can't be that. I can't be eighteen again, either. I can't get my time back.

Sometimes I start feeling sorry for myself, and I think to myself, *What a fucking rip-off.* I start to fear that I'm forgetting her, and I become guilty and angry. Other days, the memories we made feel clearer than they've ever been before. It's almost as if she's leaning over me, whispering, *Remember when . . . ?*

Frank, eighties

I met my wife, Joyce, when I was in my early thirties. We'd been together for about a year and we were going on vacation to Vienna when I asked her to marry me. I didn't ask her because she was beautiful—although she was—and I didn't ask her because I was in love with her, although I was. I asked her because she was wonderful with children. I thought to myself, *This woman will make a wonderful mother*—and she did. We've been married for over fifty years, and I don't think we've ever spent more than a few days apart. We have children and grandchildren, a comfortable home, and we lead what most people would consider to be a life of privilege.

Joyce was diagnosed with Alzheimer's a couple of months ago. I first started noticing that something was off because she was becoming uncharacteristically short-tempered with me. She started forgetting where her things were, like her car keys, and she started misplacing things altogether. I remember, once, she had put the laundry detergent in the fridge. I spent hours trying to find it. When she started showing these first signs, I lost my patience with her. I could not understand why she couldn't find her car keys all the time, or why she would say unintelligible nonsense. I yelled at her once, and I think I frightened her. I didn't know she was ill. Now that she's not there, I feel that I wasted her only chance to enjoy our last few days together.

I am a very religious man, and I became a rabbi at an early age. I have always had faith in the hand of God, but I find myself arguing with him more and more. I argue with God about my wife and why he took her beautiful mind away from her. Her illness has shaken my belief. Just about the worst thing you can experience at my age, when you're getting ready to write the last chapter of your life, is a crisis of faith. But at the same time, I have to believe in him. I have no choice—even though I cannot reconcile her illness with my faith. The Old Testament explains that Jacob mourned Joseph for over twenty years because he didn't know whether he was alive or dead. It was a terrible limbo that he felt in his heart, and that is what I feel, too. Joyce is alive, but God has taken her memories. She is an empty vessel now, and she doesn't know who I am.

It wasn't long after Joyce was formally diagnosed that the kids and I decided to move her to an assisted-living facility that's just outside the city, about a forty-five-minute drive away from our apartment. The grounds are absolutely gorgeous—lush, green, and peaceful—and the place is state-of-the-art. There's a café, a gym, a common room, a game room—there's a room for everything. The resident doctors do an amazing job overseeing and managing the needs of every patient, and the daily schedule is tailored to Joyce's particular needs. I vetted the place myself before anything was decided. Even still, I am very torn about sending Joyce there, and there isn't a day that goes by that I don't consider bringing her back home. But I can't take care of both of us. I am old myself. A couple of winters ago, I took a bad spill, and now I have trouble walking. I still drive and do my own cooking and laundry—I pride myself on being self-sufficient at my age—but doing all that and taking care of Joyce, it would be too much. I've toyed with the idea of hiring a live-in companion to help me with the chores, but mostly to keep me company. I feel very lonely. The kids all have their own families; they barely visit anymore. So I find myself eating my meals alone, going to the ballet alone.

Even though I made a very good living and continue to work, Joyce's treatments are starting to add up. I struggle to pay for everything. I wrote a letter to my representatives, telling them that it is unfair for me to have to be poor before the state will pay for my wife's assisted living. I think it should be covered by Medicare.

She's only been there for two months, and as it is, I'll run through all our savings in under a year. So there's that to worry about, too.

I visit her several times a week, and I think the people there treat her well, but it's not a good place for me to visit. I become very depressed. It's not unusual to be greeted by a screaming or crying patient, for example. There's a gentleman in his sixties there who has to have his food cut into tiny bits and fed to him by an occupational therapist because he can't even do that himself anymore. He's only a few years younger than my children! I feel like I've abandoned Joyce in hell, and I fear that in a moment of lucidity, she will recognize this.

When I went to see her one time, one of her aides asked her whether she recognized me. She said, "Yes, that's the garbage man. He's come to help me take care of the garbage." Of course, I was not offended. But I was hurt.

Another time, I heard screaming as I approached her room. It wasn't Joyce, thankfully, but her neighbor, Deb. The aides explained that Deb had refused to get dressed that morning and had hit one of the aides. Joyce witnessed it, I gathered, and she seemed really distraught in the aftermath. When we were together, she kept saying, "It's not right. It's not right to hit. They hit her. They hit Deb." I just didn't know what to make of it. It's entirely possible that her disease warped the situation and she misremembered it. But it's also possible, of course, that the aides hit Deb. You hear all sorts of horror stories, and I'm not there to protect her. I worry.

My children tell me to visit her less, but I can't seem to stay away. I go often and in the mornings, hoping that she'll give me a sign that she forgives me. If I go to see her early in the day, she's usually present, but in the afternoons, she starts sundowning—her symptoms get worse as the day wears on—and she's heartbreaking.

I love my wife, but I haven't always been a good husband to her. Joyce wanted a romantic love—a love that you see in the movies—and I couldn't give her that. I gave her the only love that made sense to me, a practical love. I provided for her, I was a good father, and for the most part, I was a good husband. I always took her with me when I traveled, we always went out to dinner, and she had free rein over spending. I was the type of man my baba had been: a family man, strong and intimidating, but somewhat distant. Once we had children, we stopped being just Joyce and just Frank—we became Mom and Dad, and that changed our marriage. So I looked for a bit of excitement elsewhere, and I had affairs; I think she suspected many and confirmed a couple throughout our marriage.

After one of my longer affairs was discovered, she left me. She moved out and abandoned me in our apartment, alone with every-thing we'd gathered throughout decades of marriage. I left the other woman almost immediately and resolved to get Joyce back. I courted her, put her first, showed her I planned to be different. But she seemed to be enjoying her independence—she was flourishing. It struck me, suddenly, that she was better off without me, that I'd been the one holding her back. Ha! And I couldn't function without her. In my life, she was indispensable, and I had taken her wholly for granted. I had been careless. It took me almost a year, but I got her back. And I was good afterward—no more affairs. I put her first, always.

I can't help but think that I contributed to her disease, though. I know I didn't, and my children tell me that I didn't. But some-times, what you think and what you feel are two very different things. When Joyce gets agitated, she becomes violent and kicks me or hits me. In those moments, I believe she knows me, she sees all the wrong that I've done, and she's doling out punishment.

A few weeks ago, Joyce had an appointment with her neurolo-gist. We went into the room together, and I helped her up onto the exam table. The doctor performed a few tests on her, the same ones she'd done times before—looked at her eyes, all that. In the mean-time, I told her that Joyce had lost a lot of weight and that I was concerned about her—concerned that perhaps she doesn't have long to live. She'd also started to walk strangely, shuffling her feet instead of picking them up. And most worrisome, she'd begun to rest her chin upon her chest, almost as if the weight of her head had become unbearable. The doctor listened patiently, and then continued with her assessment.

"Do you know who this is?" she asked, pointing to me.

"That's Frank," answered Joyce. "He's supposed to be my husband."

"Joyce," the doctor continued, "do you know the names of your children?"

Joyce shook her head.

"Do you know what month it is?"

"It's February." It was the end of December—the lobby was still decorated with garlands and lights from the holidays.

"Do you know where you are?" the doctor persisted.

"I'm in Vienna," she said, visibly flustered by the barrage of questions. Had she forgotten about our life in New York? About our kids and grandkids, too? Had her memories stalled at the beginning of our love story, all those decades ago in Vienna?

"What is this?" asked her doctor, pulling a pen from her pocket and showing it to Joyce.

"That's a pen."

"And this?" she asked, pointing to one of the buttons in her white coat.

"I can't think of the word right now," Joyce said, defeated, looking down at the floor. Hunched over the way she was, her legs dangling over the exam table, she seemed to me the young girl I'd met many years ago. Except she was no longer bold and fearless; time had worn her away little by little. I wanted nothing more at that moment than to scoop her up in my arms, to save her, to make it all okay. I wanted nothing more than to tell her she is safe with me, that I won't let anything happen to her. So much for not being one for romantic gestures. Anyhow, too little, too late.

And so it is. Sometimes my wife doesn't know who I am. She's dead and alive, and it's killing me. But, sometimes she looks at me with the love we had many years ago—when we sat together on a park bench in Vienna, she knew my name and loved me in spite of myself. And in those moments, I am glad to have that glimmer of her.

REGRET

Jane, thirties

My husband and I have been together for almost a decade, and we have one son. We met through mutual friends; he is successful, charming, and very well-liked in our circle. I would say that his guy friends almost look up to him, so much so that I'm often told that I'm "lucky" to have "found him." From the look of things, he has the perfect life and perfect family.

The thing that nobody knows about our perfect family is that my husband is a monster. He is extremely verbally abusive toward me and, on occasion, our son. He has never been physically abusive, which, I think, is why I've put up with it.

I used to be clueless as to what would send him into a tailspin, but I've become better at understanding his triggers. Sometimes, he wakes up in a mood and I can tell he's just waiting for the slightest bit of provocation to unleash on me. Other times, it's something I might say or do that upsets him. He gets quiet and brooding and secludes himself. For instance, if the three of us are spending time together and something happens, he will just go and shut himself in our bedroom without explanation. It could be hours or minutes later that he comes out and starts screaming at me.

I try to let him get it all out without interfering because I know that engaging him will just make things worse. I've spent our whole marriage walking on eggshells, afraid that the tiniest provocation will lead to another huge fight. If you were to listen to any conversation between my husband and me, I guarantee you that at least half of what I say is an iteration of "I'm sorry." I say it constantly, and it has bled into my professional life, too. I have no backbone. My first and only reaction to any situation, even one where there is no fault, is to apologize.

He is creative with his language. He says all kinds of things—tells me that I'm stupid, that I've ruined his life, that I'm a leech sucking the money out of him (I have a full-time job on top of taking care of our son), and that he made a mistake marrying me and having our son. Everything I do for this family doesn't matter. The only things that matter are his efforts. Even though I make more money than he does, he's the breadwinner. Even though I'm the primary caretaker for our son, it's my husband's contributions that seem to take precedence. I don't even dare complain about being tired at the end of a long day; he'll ask dismissively, "Why? What'd you do?"

I've heard "You're stupid" so many times that I'm starting to believe it. I don't know why I put up with it—I must be stupid, right? If I don't apologize for whatever offense he's perceived, or if I don't tell him he's right—basically, if I don't beg for forgiveness on my knees—it's a tense and horrible situation for days on end. We've spent months sleeping in separate beds—of course, I'm the one who gets banished to the guest room—and not speaking to each other, save for the weekly screaming sessions on his end. I feel like I'm holding my breath, waiting for the next round of punishment. But even when I stand my ground, what am I gaining? Eventually, things have to go back to "normal." Eventually, I have to be the one to acknowledge some sort of fault for that to happen. In the years that I've known him, he has never apologized to me.

Our son is the captive audience for this behavior—he has heard his father saying these things to his mother. I can't control when it happens, so it's impossible to preemptively remove him from the situation. I beg and plead with my husband to stop for our son's sake, but he doesn't. Sometimes, when my husband has a screaming bout in the middle of the night, our son wakes up crying and afraid. I don't know how to protect him.

In the wake of a fight, when things have calmed down, I have on occasion tried to talk to my husband about his actions. I do it in an attempt to understand why he does what he does. I've brought up things that he has said or words that he has used and confronted him with them. His defense is to deny ever saying it. If I insist, he says he doesn't remember. So then I start to think to myself: *Wait, did he actually say that? Am I misremembering?* Once, more for my own sanity than anything else, I secretly recorded one of his rants. I confronted him with the recording days later, when we were back on good terms. He completely lost his mind and started yelling at me about how recording him without his permission is illegal (it's not), and that he'll sue me and divorce me. The purpose of my actions—to show him how bad he can get when he loses his temper, since he claims to not remember—completely escaped him. It only gave him yet another reason to berate me.

I've spent so much time thinking about what could be wrong with him. He didn't grow up in a two-parent family, so I doubt he's just mimicking what he saw as a child. He is not like this with other people—at least not that I notice and not to this extent—so I don't know if he's bipolar, or has borderline personality disorder, or is depressed. I think all the hatred is coming from some sort of deep-rooted resentment that he holds against me. There was one "big love" of his life—a woman he knew before me whom he's mentioned a few times. Things didn't work out between them—that's all he's told me, and I haven't asked details because I'm not sure I want to know. Is he lashing out at me because she's the one who got away, because I remind him of the road not taken? He's always had an inflated sense of self, a really lavish idea of what his life would be. Is he upset that we've fallen short, and does he blame me for it? Our son wasn't a planned pregnancy; we actually had decided against having children. Is this all because he feels that I trapped him into parenthood? I don't know. I just don't know.

But he's a good father—a great father, when he's not in a mood. He takes our son out to activities, he's invested in his happiness and development, and he's loving. He's occasionally harder on our son when he misbehaves than I would like, but I always bear the brunt of the abuse.

The thing that scares me, though, is that after I've done damage control, he just goes back to being this normal, nice person with the snap of a finger. He can turn it off, like a switch. I wonder how one person can go from one extreme to another in a matter of seconds. When we're in the middle of one of these situations and we have to be around friends and family, he's pleasant as can be. He puts on this act for everyone and pulls me into it. It's completely psychotic. He speaks to me like he's a normal, even loving, person. He's affectionate—hugs me, puts his arm around me. And then, as soon as we're alone, he's back to his ways.

If I refuse to play along, or if someone notices that something is "up," I know I'm in for even more screaming. He blames me for making our marriage woes public and shaming us in front of friends and family. Of course, even by them I'm automatically perceived as the bad guy; my husband is too good at deceiving everyone into believing that he's this great guy.

You can set a clock by him: if a couple of good months have passed, I know he's due for a release. I feel as if he needs a place to pour all this poison building inside of him, and I'm the most convenient vessel. I can feel it coming—the little hairs on the back of my neck raise when I hear the edge in his voice—the atmosphere in the room just changes, and I know he's going to take a turn. So I start walking on eggshells, I start watching what I say, I start the placating, the coddling, the sweet talking. I think that might make it worse because he knows what I'm doing—he knows I'm trying to avoid conflict, and so I'm making it harder for him to justify a fight, not that he ever really needs justification. Eventually he'll find something, anything, and boom, we're back in hell. Just when I think I'm full, that I can't take any more of it, I find that I have more space to hold his cruelty.

I hold on because, as silly and improbable as it sounds, I forget. I forget how bad he gets. During those good months, we're a "normal" family. If he sees me working on dinner, he'll come into the kitchen and ask what he can do to help. This is the guy who screams that I am useless, that I never do anything to care for the family, that I haven't made a home-cooked meal in ages. If I have a long week at work, he will tiptoe out of the room on a Saturday morning and take our kid out so that I get to sleep in. This is the same guy who tells me that my job is cake compared to what he does. If my chronic back pain flares up, he chides me that I never follow through on physical therapy, or encourages me to take classes at our gym more often to help with recovery. And I can tell that it's out of genuine concern. This is what it's like, our life, a rhythmic swinging between extremes. It's predictable, yet arbitrary.

It's the duplicity that gets me, because it means that he knows he's being crazy and that he can control it. And I have no control— over what causes it, when it starts, when it ends, what my son will hear. So I feel very helpless, which bleeds into everything in my life. I feel powerless to change my station, powerless to fight for myself, unable to get out of bad situations. When I hear myself complain to friends and family, which I very seldom do and never about anything real that's happening in my personal life—always about something trivial, or work-related—I become tired of myself. I'm tired of the words that slip out, the feeble complaints of which nothing will come. The same shit, different day, complaining for the sake of complaint because nothing ever changes.

So, like I said, maybe he is right. I must be stupid and weak. I must deserve this life, this hatred. Because another year goes by, and I am stuck in the same hell. Which is fine. I've made my bed. But I don't even have the strength to change for my son, to get out for him. Is there anything more unforgivable?

I'm traumatized by my husband and his behavior, and I feel completely trapped in his cycle of manipulation. With him, you either bend or you break. And I've bent myself into a different person.

Terry, thirties

Charlie and I grew up together. He was my first and best friend. We bonded over the fact that our fathers were not in the picture—Charlie's refused to have anything to do with him, and I'd only ever met my real dad once or twice. We lived in a small town with nothing much to do except for hunt and fish. One time, we snuck into the dog pound and let out all the dogs. We were just kids, you know. But soon enough, we started getting into real trouble.

Charlie was a small guy, but he had unbelievable charisma; he was a womanizer and a talker. He could talk anyone into anything. I guess he still felt he had something to prove, though, because he'd always get into fights. Because I was bigger, I'd always end up getting involved to protect him. That's the type of bond we had—we had each other's back. Without question. We were closer than brothers.

I got a football scholarship in college, and my schedule filled up, so for a while it seemed like we might lose touch. He called me up one night and told me to meet him at this Chinese restaurant we used to love. He told me—point blank—that he had already robbed two pharmacies and that he was going to rob an ATM. He had a plan: one of his frat brothers knew the guy who brought the money out of the ATM machine. Charlie had stolen a dirt bike that he'd duct-taped up so that it had no identifying marks. He would punch the ATM guard, take the money, and make a getaway. He told me he needed my help.

I didn't have the stomach for these things back then, and it looked like my football career might pick up, so I refused to get involved. I got a call later that summer; he was breathing hard on the other end of the line. "I did it," he told me. And I knew exactly what he meant. Later, I saw it on TV: $28,000 in cash, stolen. Four suspects; all escaped. Charlie told me that he hid the money in the vents of the frat house and his gun in the toilet tank. He took his share, around nine grand, and spent it partying at the casino. The police eventually arrested him at his grandma's house. He went away for seven years.

In the meantime, I started working at a gym, and then my stepdad hired me into the family business. During the same few years, I met the love of my life. The same day I met her, I called my mom and I told her, "Mom, I found the one."

We wanted to experience the world before we settled down—to travel, mostly. We had these great plans. But then she went off birth control so that she could get an implant instead, and we got pregnant.

A baby was not in our plans, but we kept on coming back to the feeling that maybe it was meant to be. Maybe the universe was giving us a sign. So we decided to keep the baby and got married two years after she was born. But then my stepdad died suddenly. My mom was a mess. I inherited the burden of the family businesses, but I knew almost nothing about running a business, and I started struggling.

The stresses of being a parent and running a big business got to me. I started taking OxyContin. It was stupidly easy to get a hold of, and I only needed to work two doctors. They both knew that I played football in college. I'd just tell them that my knee hurt or my back hurt, and they'd write me a script, no questions asked. No offense, but I just don't look like a junkie, so they never suspected a thing. And—as it happens in the perfect storm—Charlie got out of prison.

He'd met a few like-minded people inside, and he was back to his old ways almost immediately. I gave him a small loan of $5,000 so that he could get back on his feet, and I tried to keep my hands clean. I even offered to let him move in with us while he got his bearings. But the drugs started taking their toll on me. Neither my wife nor my mom knew that I was using, and I wasn't strong enough to stop on my own. Pain pills take all the pain away—physically, mentally, everything. And when you're going through so much, they're an outlet. I wanted to stop so many times, but my body wouldn't let me.

I started slipping up. I worked the referrals that my dad had left behind at one of the businesses, and I got us a bunch of new contracts. But I made mistakes and cost the company $10,000, which wasn't a huge deal financially. It was our reputation that took a big hit. Thank God my mother had the good sense to sell all the other businesses. We got into a fight because I wanted to keep them—I was so strung out that I wasn't seeing the truth.

Eventually, I lost the one business we hadn't sold, and my wife found out about my drug problem. We were drinking together one night and got into a physical fight when I told her the truth. She called the cops on me. I went to jail for four days, and I felt like absolute shit about what I'd done. My real dad was an abuser, and I punished myself mentally for turning out like him, the piece-of-shit wife beater my mom told me about. When I got out, I apologized, but it was too late. She'd been unhappy for a long time, and I was high all the time, so I hadn't seen it. She started divorce proceedings. Before long, I was homeless, and Charlie had my back. I moved in with him and his girlfriend. And that's when I started to dabble in heroin.

Charlie and his girl got into a lot of illegal things, and I turned a blind eye while we were living together. At that point, he had become my dealer, too—and so long as I got my fix, I didn't really care what they were doing. But I saw too much, and I started getting scared. He was dealing with serious people—he met this Mexican dude in prison who was associated with a cartel. The guy moved in with us and started bringing in a bunch of heroin, meth, Molly—anything you could think of, but mostly huge blocks of heroin. They'd keep half of it to deal themselves, and the rest went out to other dealers in the city.

Once my divorce was settled, I wanted to make sure that I got shared custody of my daughter, so I moved out of the drug den and got my own place. The drugs had transformed me physically—I'd lost a lot of weight, and my face had broken out—but I still looked like I had it together. I've been pulled over by cops and had a bunch of drugs on me, but the cops never bothered to check. I just don't look like the type. So I was living this perfect double life. It was time for me to shape up, though, for my kid's sake, so I went on methadone and got a job. I focused on my new job and being a dad, but I kept in touch with Charlie. We would get together once a week, hang out in Charlie's kitchen, look up recipes online, and make dinner. I mean, if you didn't know about the pounds of drugs all over the house, we were kind of the perfect picture of male friendship. And I was doing well for a while.

But the job ended up not working out. I was working nights, and it screwed my schedule up with my daughter. I got hired away to another gig and was making okay money, but I fell off the wagon and got back on heroin. In the meantime, the cartel dealer had become a totally different person—violent, scary, unpredictable—you didn't want to be around him anymore. He got pulled over and arrested for a traffic violation, but the cops didn't know he had five grams of heroin in his stomach. He feigned illness, and they took him to a hospital, where he threw the drugs up and hid them in the bathroom ceiling tile. When they took him to jail, he used his phone call to let Charlie know where the drugs were.

All of his dealings put Charlie on the DEA's radar, and eventually the law caught up with him. They raided his place and charged him with "conspiracy to commit trafficking," I think it was. He needed money for his defense attorneys and I needed money to pay off the lawyer after my divorce, so we switched up our game. We came up with this grand scheme of hitting up storage units and stealing from them, bit by bit, so that the owners wouldn't notice. We'd sell everything online through eBay or Craigslist, and we were making a lot of money. We went high-tech with it—bought drones so that we could see if cops were coming, signal jammers, blankets that muted our body heat in case they were using infrared technology to surveil the area. My hands definitely weren't clean anymore. And we were doing heroin still; I mean, to do all of this stuff, you definitely have to be on something.

The storage units were a gold mine. One in particular was worth thousands of dollars. We kept hitting it up over the span of a few months, and we realized that the owner must have been a collector. We saw a license that he'd left in the unit—he was this old guy with white hair. We ended up finding him, actually. He lived in a retirement community, alone. No family. He was probably paying for his housing with what he had in that unit. It was probably his life's savings. My conscience finally kicked in, and I couldn't do it anymore. I told Charlie I wanted out. He told me he wanted to hit up this guy's condo. "That's probably where he keeps all the really good stuff," was his theory. Storage units felt impersonal to me, but people's homes—no, I couldn't do it. But Charlie went ahead on his own. He got greedy. He didn't know when to stop.

Charlie and his girl started hitting up homes and units multiple times a week. We fell out of touch for about three months, then he showed up on my doorstep one night and asked to stay with me. I opened my door to him, as I always had. I came home from work the next day and it was clear the place had been tossed. Charlie called me and asked if the police were still there—I said they'd left. But to tell you the truth, I felt betrayed that he knew the cops had been there and he didn't give me a heads-up.

The DEA and the state Bureau of Investigation came back the next day and told me my friend was wanted for trafficking heroin, Molly, and meth, and for robbing storage units and homes. I acted shocked. They suggested that I could be implicated in the crimes if I didn't help them track Charlie down. So I called him and told him I needed my fix even though it had been a while since I was regularly getting high—but I wanted to tip him off, so I called him by a nickname that we hadn't used since high school. He picked up on it, I think, and he said something that has stayed with me to this day. He said, "Oh, man, I haven't heard from you in forever." And he said it a few times, as if he was trying to clear me, to make sure that the cops knew I didn't have any part in this.

It took a few tries—Charlie was always slick—but eventually, and with my help, the cops got him. I was with him that day. He pulled over in a Barnes & Noble parking lot to let me out, and he said, "Hey, it's been good knowing ya." I called the DEA agent and let him know where Charlie was heading, and they got him.

He's serving thirty years in prison. He'll be sixtysomething when he gets out. I've always felt guilty about what I did, like I betrayed my own brother. But also kind of relieved. I couldn't risk getting caught up in it. I am clean now—have been for over a year—and I see my daughter as often as I can. I have a good job. I feel like I got a second chance, so I'm trying not to throw it away. But, man, the past weighs on me.

George, sixty-five

I'm in my apartment for 95 percent of my life. I only go out for food and medicine, and that's only if I can't get it delivered, or if I need it urgently. When I do get food, I shop for the whole month. All in all, I usually end up having around eighty-five bags. I've had my car for nine years, and it only has about forty thousand miles on it. I've done the math, and that amounts to about twelve miles a day. On days that I don't feel well, which is the vast majority of my days, that's definitely an overestimate.

I wash my clothes once or twice a year. This year—let's see, it's March—so I've only showered twice. The longest I've ever gone without a shower is ninety-six days. It's usually the case that something triggers the shower, like cutting the grass or something like that. But I brush my teeth three times a day and I put deodorant on. I'm not really concerned about whether I smell, because I'm seldom around people. If company ever finds me, I keep my distance. But that's rare, you know, and I'm okay with it because I don't much like people. Plus, when I'm not feeling good, I don't have the ability to make people laugh, and so I become very self-conscious and I isolate. The people who come to see me regularly in the last few years are my landlord (to pick up checks), and the delivery guy (to drop off food or packages, and pick up checks). Basically, all I'm good for is the money.

I only eat off paper plates and drink from plastic cups. I try to reuse as much as I can, but I realize it's wasteful. I don't know what to do—if I used real plates, I don't think I'd ever get around to washing them. I look around my apartment and it's easy to become overwhelmed—the sink, the trash can, the kitchen counters, are all overflowing with stuff, garbage. In one corner of my living room,

I've piled up cardboard boxes from mail deliveries. I keep the boxes in case I ever need to mail anything out—that way I don't have to pay extra for packaging. Sometimes, I'll go months without taking out the garbage, which is useful because I need all the Gatorade bottles I can get.

When I go out to shop, I usually buy the thirty-two-ounce bottles of Gatorade that I then line up by my bed. Once I'm done drinking the Gatorade, I pee in the bottles so that I don't have to get out of bed. Sometimes, I'm so depressed that I don't get out of bed for weeks on end, and when I feel better, I notice that I've gotten bedsores.

It was during one of the long stretches of depression that I ran out of free bottles, so I ended up peeing in a half-full orange-flavored bottle. Needless to say, I forgot about it the next day, and it took two full gulps for me to realize that I was drinking my own piss. Which, when you really think about it, is kind of funny. Or at least I thought it was.

I don't think I'm a hoarder. I'm not a hoarder. It's hard to get around my apartment because there's lots of garbage that I don't throw out fast enough, but that's not because I want to keep it. I mostly just can't get up the courage to go down to the dumpster.

I wasn't always like this. I mean, I was married for twelve years and I had children, but over the years I was just defeated by depression. My depression was left undiagnosed for too long, and when it finally was, it wasn't treated well, so the way I look at it is: it was allowed to fester inside me. I jettisoned parts of my life that I could no longer deal with—that took too much time or effort—and eventually I was left with the basic necessities. My illness, my depression, it raped my self-esteem, my ambition, my thirst to live. Over thirty years of paring down my life has taught me that there are very few things that one actually needs.

Here's what I need: I need food, drink, and a cozy place to sleep. I need companionship, and it's fine if it's digital—I like ESPN better than I like most people. I need to occasionally check in with my kids so that I know that they are okay. And that's about it. Everything else is very disposable. I used to think I needed the latest gadgets, a nice car, nice clothes for work, enough money for a membership at a country club. But then I think I realized that instead of adding enjoyment to my life, these things were just adding stress. Keeping up with the Joneses is a lot of work when something is broken inside. So I lost everything, little by little, and imagine my surprise when nothing much changed. It was liberating. Solitude is freedom.

I feel bad for my ex-wife. Being married to me, especially toward the end, must have been very challenging. She tried her best, but my depression dragged both of us down. I wasn't communicating. I was totally isolating myself from her, and she didn't know how to get through to me. My generation, we don't know very much about mental health, and that's a big disservice to us. I've been this way, I've struggled with my mental health, for as long as I can remember. It's not like it hit me in middle age. But it fell through the cracks. I didn't know how to communicate about it, certainly not with my wife but not with my doctor, either, and so I wrote it off and I put it off. Whether it's ignorance, machismo, or just a generational thing, I don't know. But I wasn't raised to complain, and my own father didn't believe in doctors and such—unless you were missing a limb, you were likely fine. So by the time I realized something needed to be done, there were casualties: my marriage, my home, the family we'd built.

I don't have any responsibilities anymore. I took care of my family financially, I'm self-sufficient, and I'm not doing anyone any harm. My biggest everyday concern is whether I have enough to eat and whether today is the day I will be found dead in my apartment. I don't have cats, so at least I know I won't be partially eaten when I'm found. That may sound morbid, but it's a practical concern for someone like me. So I suppose I'm just waiting around to die. All the men in my family passed away before the age of sixty-two of a heart attack, and I'm sixty-five, so . . . I guess it could happen at any time, and that's as scary as it is exciting to me. I had a heart attack a few years ago, but I survived it. I'm a ticking time bomb, you could say. I have a funeral plan that's all paid for, I have an executor to my will, and I save a little bit of money every month so that I can leave my kids something when I go.

I take a fistful of pills every day—twenty pills, to be exact—for depression, bipolar disorder, and my heart. They basically bury my sex drive under six feet of concrete, but Viagra still overrides them, sometimes. There's a woman I know who also struggles with depression, and she's on a lot of medicine, too. She comes over every once in a while. We make the most out of it. We get out of it what we can. She's from Peru. She visits her family there often, and that's where she gets the Viagra. I guess it's cheaper there, or something.

In terms of indulgences, let's see . . . I have a pair of furry slippers that I love. I spend all day in those slippers, and the soles are coming off, but they're mine and I love them. The downstairs neighbor has two dogs that he lets me play with. He and I get along sports-wise. I'm on eBay a lot. I buy myself things that make me briefly feel better—mostly collectibles that aren't worth anything. It's not really about the things themselves but about the feeling I get when I'm expecting mail. It's exciting, a good change in my routine. Retail therapy, as they say. I sell some stuff, too, but that requires a lot of effort—I have to take photos, post it online, etc. It's too much work, so mostly I end up piling things up in a corner somewhere.

I am alone a lot, but I don't really get bored. I watch a lot of television because it helps keep my mind occupied and it's my lifeline to the outside world. Sometimes I need the rush I get from hearing another voice in the apartment, even if it's from the television. I need that constant companionship because I just never know when I'll take a turn. My depression can hit me any time and any place—in the middle of sex—it used to even happen when I was out riding the motorcycle. And I have something the doctors called ultra-rapid cycling bipolar disorder, which is a fancy way of saying that I have very frequent mood changes. There's only one thing that ends the episode: somewhere between twenty-two to twenty-three hours of being awake during an episode of hypomania, I can force myself to sleep from exhaustion. And then I'm back to plain old depression. It's like a reset button.

I haven't seen my daughter in over ten years. I call her on the phone about once a year; I used to call more but she told me to stop, so now we try to email about once a month. She's limited me to once a month, and I can only send her funny things that I find on the Internet. I haven't seen my son or spoken to him in over two years. Last time we spoke, he told me that he doesn't have room in his life for negative people and negative relationships. Listen, I understand. I wouldn't want to have me as a dad, either. My kids have their own lives, their own worries. I'm sure they'd rather not have to worry about me, too, and on the phone I'm bound to say something that makes them add me to their mental to-do list. So they keep me at arm's distance. I'm a bit of a downer.

But I like myself and how I do things, I guess. Life is easier now that I've accepted my disease. I can't beat it, so I've adapted to it. The way I look at it, I have few regrets. I fulfilled my responsibilities as a husband and father. I went on a few adventures. Hey, I lived a full life.

Now, I wait.

Raven, twenty-nine

One of my earliest memories is of some guy pushing his way into our apartment, undoing his belt buckle, and sliding his jeans halfway down his legs as he handed my mother a fistful of cigarettes. This was my signal to go to the kitchen and return only once my mother had started smoking on our worn-out couch. Sometimes she would remember to call me back in. Most times, she forgot. I'd take little peeks through the opening that separated the kitchen from the rest of the apartment, so I saw a lot of things that I had no business seeing.

Probably one of the first lessons I learned as a kid was that I couldn't count on my mother to remember to feed me, to help with homework, or to wake me up for school. If I wanted to do any of that, it was up to me. And if I didn't, well, that was up to me, too. I was always the adult. So, I'd remind her when we were running low on groceries and if we had the money, I'd throw in a small bag of Lay's chips as a treat to myself while we waited in the checkout line. My favorite flavor was salt and vinegar because I liked the way the vinegar would make the sides of my mouth pruney.

Most of all, though, I couldn't count on my mom to protect me. I always had an eye on her. She needed taking care of, but when it most mattered, she wasn't there to take care of me. So, it was only a matter of time before those men who were coming in and out of the apartment got their hands on me, too.

My mom had me when she was seventeen. I had my own daughter when I was eighteen, a senior in high school. I wasn't ready to be a mom. I still wanted to smoke and drink. I actually don't think I ever wanted kids—I might have made a nice godparent, but that's about it. My daughter's father was sixteen or seventeen, a sophomore. He was studious and preppy, and he was holding down a job even then. He worked at a fast-food chain, and he was there when I called him and told him I was pregnant. In my high school, lots of girls got pregnant, so we didn't really treat it like it was a big deal. I mean, it was common; we didn't trip.

I had my daughter and left her with her father. I had the opportunity to go off to college; my dad dropped me off with $100, and I didn't hear anything from him for years. Turns out, he got locked up for seven years for selling drugs. He recently got paroled. I heard through other people that he took a deal to snitch on my uncle, who is also in the business. I'm not sure, though. We're not in touch.

Well, I never ended up graduating from college. I gave up somewhere along the way and decided, if I die tomorrow, I'm going to do what I wanna do today. And what I wanted to do was PCP. The first time I smoked PCP, I told myself that I was just experimenting and I'd stop whenever I wanted. It looked just like a cigarette, but it stank. Some guy sold it to me for $20 a pop. Soon enough, I was smoking two or three sherms a day, and I figured out that I could get it for $15 "if they liked me"—meaning, if I got on my knees and made it worth their while. And before I knew it, I'd become my mother—passed out on a couch, wetted out.

Being on PCP is like being on a movie set, or like being on vacation. There's a sense of lightness—a suspension of reality. I felt carefree, powerful, superhuman. Above it all. One night, after I'd smoked, I decided to walk from my apartment to the 7-Eleven on the corner for a Slurpee and some Cheetos. I saw three men standing outside one of the concrete buildings to my left. Then, one started running toward me. I felt like I was walking so quickly that we would collide. But then, as if someone had lassoed him, he stopped abruptly and fell to the ground. When I reached him, I looked down at him: his eyes were open, glassy. I didn't feel anything at all. I looked back at the two other men. They were there, and then they weren't. After standing over him for what could have been a second or half an hour, I kept walking to the 7-Eleven. I could have done something. I could have called an ambulance or given him CPR. Maybe I could have saved his life. But I was in video-game mode. Nothing sank in, nothing got to me.

Actually, thinking back on this, I'm not even sure it's a real memory. Maybe I hallucinated it.

A large part of these years is very hazy, in between reality and dream world. I was doing what I needed to do to get to the next high, and not much else. To fuel my addiction, I started writing bad checks and stealing credit cards, and eventually it caught up with me. I was held at the county correctional facility for two weeks. I got through the detox, which was absolutely brutal. It's like all the pain and shit you've been getting high to avoid gets dumped on you all at once. Then they moved me to an out-of-state prison for four months. I felt really unsafe there. I was around so many dope fiends, and people with hep C or HIV. My bunkmate was a fifty-two-year-old woman with a colostomy bag that she changed in the middle of the night. It smelled awful. When I was there, it was just about survival. Let me put it this way: you don't hear any happy stories. Everybody's got something they went through—someone beat them, someone didn't love them, whatever. So you find someone whose something looks a little like yours, and you band together to get through it.

When I got out, I went back to my old ways almost immediately. These were my days of turning tricks. I had a lot of stripper friends, and pretty soon, stripper logic started making a lot of sense to me. Basically, "If you're going to fuck, don't do it for free." I started charging about $200 for thirty minutes, and slept with over one hundred people in a matter of two or three months. I used to think—*it'll be over soon, and then I can smoke and drink and be in control of my body again.*

I always used protection but, honestly, it was dirty business. The worst was this guy who was a big-time lawyer. He was in his fifties but didn't look it at all—he barely looked a day over thirty. But he was fat and something about him gave off the impression that he was a slob. I think it was the way that he ate: sloppily, noisily, messily. His house was also absolutely disgusting. One time, we drank a whole fifth of Rémy and had sex. His penis was tiny; the condom didn't even fit. He kept trying to kiss me, and it made my stomach turn over. Kissing is intimate, too intimate. People don't know how to do it well, and you can't have a protected kiss. But he was all over me, and I figured—what's the point of resisting? The good thing about this particular guy was that he made me feel so demeaned that I stopped turning tricks. That experience messed with me. He was the last person I slept with for money. And once the money ran out, my drug habit did, too.

I got myself together and got a job at a local chain restaurant. I've been promoted a bunch of times, up to managerial positions. It's not my cup of tea—I mean, it's definitely not what I had dreamed of doing with my life—but I can build from it. I met my girlfriend, who is very loving and supportive. I was attracted to her mind, and I fell in love with the person, not the gender. She helped rebuild me, which is a good thing, because I wasn't a fan of the old me.

The old me did a couple of friends dirty. I slept with their boyfriends and took money from them for sex. At the time, I was telling myself that I was doing them a favor: if a man doesn't claim you by putting a ring on it, it's fair game. The old me all but abandoned my daughter. Before her father won custody, she was being raised by strangers. He has had her for four years now. I see her every once in a while, but we never bonded. She's better off. I spared her having to be raised by someone like me.

I guess what's really scary is how much the old me reminds me of my mother. I used to think back to when I saw her lying on that couch, unconscious, with a parade of men coming in and out of the apartment doing whatever they damn well pleased to me and her. I didn't know better than to accept it as an okay life to live. That's all I ever saw: drugged-out mother, jailed father. When that's your starting point, how far can you really get in life? How much of a chance do you really stand?

Lucas, forty-one

I was twenty-five years old when I went to prison and forty when I was released.

I am one of five children. I grew up in a rough neighborhood and lived in the projects. My mother was college-educated, but her husband got her hooked on drugs. Ever since fourth grade, I've been trying to make money, go to school, and feed everyone. I've always known how to fend for myself.

When I got arrested, I was working and going to school full-time. I had a four-year-old son. I was a first-time, nonviolent offender accused of interfering with a federal investigation. I worked for the housing authority, so I had access to when they'd be doing drug raids. The Feds accused me of leaking information and added on a conspiracy-to-sell-crack-cocaine charge; I guess the people allegedly benefiting from my insider information had a pretty extensive drug operation. The Feds pressured me to snitch—to give up whatever information I might have known about illegal activity in public housing. I didn't refuse due to some misguided loyalty. I refused because I didn't actually know anything. At trial, there was no evidence against me. They dismissed the charge for interfering with a federal investigation but convicted me of one count of conspiracy to sell crack cocaine. I'm a young black man from the projects, so the verdict came back in a heartbeat: a 240-month sentence in a federal prison. As far as I'm concerned, that's a lifetime.

The first two years in prison were really stressful. I was in denial. Prison life is really hard to adjust to—you have all this extra energy in the beginning, and nothing to do with it. You eat what they give you. You sleep when they tell you. You go only where you're allowed. You're basically cattle. It hadn't clicked yet that this would be what the next twenty years of my life would look like. I developed high blood pressure and had several stress-related breakdowns. Over the years, I was transferred to seven different federal facilities. Twice, it was for disciplinary reasons. In some places, I was the one who was feared; in others, it was my turn to be afraid.

When I was in Arizona, there were race riots. The Mexicans and the blacks didn't get along. The guards had absolutely no control over the prisoners. In other prisons, the guards run the show—I've seen a lot of dirty guards, just people who go mad with the power bestowed on them. They pit the prisoners against each other for fun, just to see what happens. A lot of the guys took their time breaking up fights, but all it takes is a couple of seconds to shank someone to death. You find out the hard way, too, that it's a small world. A lot of inmates end up doing time with people they might have had bad blood with on the outside.

Other than the constant existential threat, prison life is really regimented: lights go out at 10:30 p.m. and on at 5:30 a.m. every day. Your bed needs to be made perfectly, and they have a little cartoon of what it should look like when you're done. You get fed at 6:00 a.m. The food depends on the facility—the federal prison system has good meals, and sometimes you can even cook your own food. Then you have work call from 7:00 a.m. to 2:30 p.m. I got paid six cents an hour. Then you get to work out. You shower. You get ready for count at 4:00 p.m. and 10:00 p.m. In between, you can watch TV—they have basic cable, so you can watch ESPN and TV shows. The inmates control the TVs themselves based on seniority. There's a recreational area, an arts and crafts room, and a library, too. And you learn a few tricks along the way—how to get kites (messages) out to people, how to make "pruno" or "juice" (alcohol), how to get things past the guards, how to barter commissary. Prisoners are creative, man. It takes a while, but you start to get comfortable. If you mind your business and behave, life is almost . . . pleasant. Basically, you're on autopilot.

But if you sleep in and you miss your work detail too often, they put you in segregation or give you extra duties. If you do anything that's considered an infraction of prison rules, you get a "shot." A one-hundred-series shot is a big deal—maybe you jumped someone and seriously wounded him—and you would usually get transferred to a higher security prison, and it would go on your record and take about ten years to clear. A two-hundred-series shot is borderline; you get that if you get into a fight with someone, and it means you get commissary, phone, and visitation privileges taken away. A three-hundred-series shot is not serious; you'd get one for insolence, unauthorized contraband, or being late to work. Four-hundred-series shots are basically never given out. Just when you start to think that things aren't so bad, the guards remind you where you are. They can make life hard, push you around, make you feel unsafe—they're part of the problem.

The people who make trouble are always the ones who have the shorter sentences. Prisoners with two or three life sentences are humble and respectful, in my experience. They've accepted their fates: they're going to die in prison. I have no idea whether this is actually true, but prison lore has it that the sentencing computation or custody classification forms for the lifers just say "deceased" on them. For many of the prisoners, both lifers and short-term, though, prison life is better than being at home.

My first day out, I had butterflies in my stomach and I felt nauseous. I ended up serving a little over fifteen years of my twenty-year sentence. I was happy and angry at the same time. The judge took forever to hand down the order of release. I missed my bus and ended up having to wait over twelve hours in a Greyhound station. I felt like the noise and commotion was going to swallow me up. It took me two full days to get where I needed to be. I kept looking around, wondering if an officer was going to come and take me back.

When I finally got to my home state, two probation officers—a man and a woman—came and took me clothes shopping at a place called Forman Mills. It's basically the cheapest store out there. I got a coat, some jeans, and a pair of slippers. I was ashamed when we were walking around the store because it was obvious that they were law enforcement. But the lady officer was actually really nice; she was very motherly toward me. She would put shirts up to my chest in their hangers, cock her head sideways, and look at me like she cared—like she really cared—if the $5 shirt looked good on me or not. You notice things like that after fifteen years of being nobody. They put me up in a motel for a few days, until I could get back on my feet. I signed with a staffing agency, but I haven't had much luck.

When you're in prison for so long, you become accustomed to living without real responsibilities. You don't pay rent or bills, and you're provided with three meals a day. You pay commissary or whatever debt you may have caused, but that's it. Also, it's not as dangerous in prison as it is on the streets—at least, not for a black man. Most importantly, people have your back. You learn who to trust and count on, you learn who is reliable and keeps his mouth shut, you learn who'll snitch. There's prison justice, you know. People get theirs, eventually, and there's something comforting about that. That's what's missing on the outside—the outside is cruel. It doesn't care if you did the crime or you deserved your punishment, or you served your time. To them, you're always going to be a prisoner, no matter what. I get a little self-conscious about it; I feel like it's written on my forehead, like everybody knows.

While I was gone, my father and grandmother died. My son grew up seeing his father behind bars. He's twenty years old now. He was four when I went in. When he was eighteen, he came to visit me in prison and we had a talk. I think as he's gotten older, he understands the systemic issues behind my incarceration. But still: he has barely had me in his life, and because we live in separate states and I'm on probation, I can't go to see him.

I'm struggling to take care of myself, and I'm really lonely. I had become accustomed to sleeping in those narrow beds, facing a concrete wall. Now, there's too much space, too much air around me.

It's suffocating. Sleep doesn't come easy anymore. That's one of the hardest adjustments.

One of the traps that people fall into is that they spend a lot of time imagining what life is going to be like when they're free, and then they're not only disappointed, but they're disappointed to the extent that they start missing being locked up. Without some sort of cornerstone for life on the outside, it's really easy to get lost, really easy to feel overwhelmed. I don't have a very good support system out here. My sisters came down to visit me from Ohio right after I was released, and it was nice to see them, but what can they do? They have their own lives, their kids, their responsibilities. They don't have time for me.

I need to make money to live, and I can't do that if nobody will employ me. This is why so many people end up back behind bars: if the choice is between survival and crime, most people would pick crime. Now that I am back on the bottom, I'm afraid I won't be able to dig myself out. What I'm most afraid of is the little voice in the back of my head that tells me it wouldn't be so bad if I landed back in prison, after all. I think: *What would I do for security? And food, and work, and ESPN?* And sometimes I think: *What could I do—what can I get into so that I can go back?* Funny enough, it's an escape fantasy.

It's hard to believe that I'm a free man now. Because there's a difference between free and freed. I don't really feel free. I still get out of bed at the same time every morning and eat at the same time as when I was inside. I make up my bed the same way I used to, too. I catch myself looking above the headboard for the cartoon instructions. Sometimes you just need a little validation that you're doing the right thing, even if it's just making the bed.

Sarah, midforties

I was going to let it go on until it killed me. From the time I woke up to the moment I went to sleep, it's all I thought about. Every single thing I did was for one purpose alone: getting a fix. You know those stories that people always tell about some person they once knew who has the craziest stories? It always happens to the other guy, but I feel like I've been through it all. I am the other guy.

I started getting high and drinking with my mom's third husband. He would ply me with booze and weed because it made me more submissive—easier to control when he molested me. I knew that what he was doing was wrong, but he threatened to hurt my younger sister whenever I resisted. So, in my mind, I was sacrificing myself for her sake. I'll never forget the moment, years later, when she told me that she used to be jealous of all the time that "Daddy" spent with me. She had no idea, and I never directly told her.

My real father was drunk when he died. He must have been in his early twenties, and I was barely three. Both sets of grandparents had substance-abuse issues, too. My mom was clean, though. Her whole life, she held down several jobs to keep her kids fed, dressed, and in school. But we all turned out a mess in our own ways. Addiction definitely ran in the family. They say that it's a disease—like cancer. Well, this was a cancer that was growing inside me ever since I was born. I feel like I don't remember a life in which alcohol and drugs weren't everywhere.

I had two kids in the 1980s, but even then my addiction showed no signs of slowing down. The guy I was dating back then—we used together. We stole and pawned things off to support our habit. We had a dealer who would pick out things from the Macy's catalog—back in those days, Tommy Hilfiger was having a moment.

We would boost whatever he wanted from the store, and he would pay us in dope. We just needed enough money for the fix, and on good days, we made enough to sleep indoors.

We had a usual spot—a filthy motel room that only cost us a few bucks because we knew the owner. I think he felt bad for the kids. One night, we had just gotten the dope, and I was getting ready to shoot. This was my addiction at its worst—my veins were all dead, and I was bleeding from infected sores on my arms, my feet, my legs, my stomach, and my chest. I was having trouble finding a good vein; I got a flash, but then I lost the vein and couldn't find it again. I wasted the dope.

I got so frenzied. I started panicking, screaming, pacing, and jumping on things. I didn't know what to do. And then I caught a glimpse of myself in the hotel mirror, and it was horrific. I remember thinking—*that's not me; that doesn't even look like me.* And even now when I think back on this moment, it feels like it happened to someone else and I witnessed it. It helps me to think of it that way, because if I felt everything, I would crumble.

I wanted to be a good mom, and I tried. The love I have for my children is more powerful than anything I've ever encountered, except my addiction. My addiction made me feel like I was always behind the eight ball, always playing catch-up, always fixing something I'd messed up with the kids. I wanted to stay clean, but something inevitably went wrong, and I didn't have healthy coping mechanisms or a support network, and getting high was the escape. I felt that I'd already messed up so much—hey, what's another time? One last time. That's why they call it a "fix"—you're chasing an alternate reality, a world in which whatever happened to fuck you up is erased, fixed.

On bad days—and yes, it got worse—we slept in parking lots. I remember one night we had the kids with us, and we had just settled in a Babies R Us parking lot. My youngest child was very ill, and it started pouring rain outside. I started to get us all under that big blue awning, but I couldn't move very well because I had open sores on my feet. My youngest was clutching on to my hand, and then all of a sudden he dropped to the ground and started having a seizure. I didn't know what to do—I just stood there, crying, screaming at God.

What scares me is that even that wasn't enough for me to quit. I was in and out of jail, in and out of rehab, in and out of hospitals—probably more times than I can count on all my fingers and toes. The last time I was admitted to a hospital, the doctor took a look at my toxicology report and told me that there was "a little bit of blood in my drug stream." He told me I was going to die, and I believed him.

I met my now-husband when I was working nights as a stocker at a big grocery store. I bummed a cigarette from him—and eventually we started using together. Finally, almost a decade ago today, he came up to me and told me he was getting clean or he was dying, and that if I wanted to be with him, I had to help him live. Who would have thought it, huh, that a great love story could be behind all of this? But that's what we have: a great love. He is always supportive of me, always good to me, even when I don't deserve it. And we keep each other up; we keep each other going every day. When he has bad days, I am strong for him. When I have bad days, he is strong for me.

You'd think that after almost ten years, it gets easier. You'd think that the draw fades a little bit, that your brain starts to forget how good it felt to float away—to be vacant, forget the past, forget the ugly—for a few hours. But it's still difficult. I think it will always be difficult, even when I'm gray and old and the scars have blended in with the wrinkles. I have to remind myself every single day that I don't want to throw away a decade of sobriety.

The hardest part is my relationship with my children. I'm very close with the oldest, but the youngest and I aren't on the best terms. They spent most of their childhoods with their grandmother, who provided them with stability and a roof over their heads. Their memories of me aren't exactly good. My oldest told me a few days ago that he remembers me showing up to his birthday party and throwing up in the bushes in front of his friends.

I remember that a strong midday sun illuminated the backyard and the kids were swarming around loudly, chasing one another in and out of the house. It was summer in the 1980s. The kids were staying with their grandmother on a semipermanent basis at that point, but I went over to visit when I could. I started to feel sick, like the sun was burning off my skin and I was overheating. I felt like I might pass out, but I was trying to hold it together for the sake of the kids. I'd been trying to get clean, so I hadn't used that morning.

My timing really couldn't have been any worse. My mom was bringing out the cake and everyone started singing "Happy Birthday." I lunged out of my chair and went headfirst into the bushes. It was all I could do to keep myself from throwing up on the table, in front of all the children. My mom kicked me out after that—and I went to shoot up.

I had completely forgotten about this particular incident until he brought it up, but my son remembered it like it was yesterday. I can only imagine what else I did, how else I scarred my kids, what else they've seen. How can I make amends for something when I can't remember such a big part of it? I don't blame them if they want nothing to do with me. It's hard to ever feel clean after everything I've done. Some things you can't forget—no matter how many drugs you're on. Sometimes, I feel like I'm being punished. But I can't hold it against my children, because I also feel that I deserve the punishment.

I wanted my kids to have what I didn't have—a safe childhood, opportunities, a steady job, and parents who love them. I've probably played the biggest role in them not getting that. They're both so smart, so brilliant, so kind, but they are these things in spite of me. And I am afraid—every single day—that I passed my disease on to them. I would never forgive myself.

I'm starting to make peace with some of the ugly things I did. I'm talking to the people I've hurt and understanding their side of the story. I'm piecing together almost two decades of heroin addiction and seeing my life for the first time as a sober person. It's taken a lot of work to understand my addiction and what fueled it, and to let go of the things that weren't in my control. I'm turning it around—not just for me, but for my kids, too.

Sometimes I walk along the neighborhoods where I used to score, and I look at these new fancy restaurants and businesses that have opened up. There's a tapas place on the corner where my dealer used to hang out. Now it's crowded by yuppies on their lunch break. The streets don't remember—it seems that the world has moved on. Every day, I have to wake up, cover my scars, and pretend that I have, too.

Shep, midforties

I make $2,500 every two weeks, after taxes, working somewhere in the ballpark of a sixty-hour week. Of that money, $1,700 goes to my first ex-wife, with whom I have a son and a daughter, for child support. No word yet on how much of my paycheck will go to my soon-to-be second-ex-wife, for more child support. I'm in my midforties, I don't own my home—not for lack of trying—and my bank balance, after I get paid and before I pay the bills, reads -$1,200.

The rapid descent started, I guess, in 2016. My second wife and I had been married for a few years. She'd been going to school to become a massage therapist, and I supported her financially through it. It took three years, and it was like pushing an elephant up a hill with a feather, but she finally graduated and established a steady clientele. She was making good money, and things started looking up for us.

We talked about it and decided to start trying to have a baby. Of course, a heartbeat later, she was pregnant. The house I had bought—a $272,000 investment on which I still owe $222,000 after almost ten years of payments (high interest, zero money down, forty-year mortgage)—was starting to fall apart. There were 252 broken tiles on the main floor. There was no way I would bring this little guy into a world with crawling hazards.

I slowly started repairing the main floor, by myself, after work. I couldn't do it while my wife was awake and about, because the fumes from the chemicals could hurt her and the baby. So I fixed most of it between the hours of 10:00 p.m. to 3:00 a.m., during which she slept in our bedroom. At 6:00 a.m., I'd wake up to go to work. With a schedule like that, naturally we didn't get to see very much of each other, and I could tell that it was putting her on edge.

She seemed very sensitive and distant, but I chalked it up to the stress of the pregnancy and did my own brand of nesting: I tried to get the house pristine, ready and safe for the baby. But I told my wife, "No matter what's happening, you can always come talk to me; I'm always here for you."

I got home from work one day—June 3, a Tuesday. I found her in the bedroom, crying, and she admitted to cheating on me.

And then she said, "But that's not the worst of it. I've been reported at work, and I'm going to be fired, lose my license, and have to pay a fortune in fines."

I asked her how many times she slept with him, and she said once. To confirm, I looked through her billing—she was a contractor and had to keep her own records—and she'd been seeing this guy an average of thirteen times a month for the last nine months. His wife had found text messages that he'd erased on his phone and called the local board that regulates massage therapists to report my wife. My wife was a little smarter about it—she came clean and told me she had downloaded some sort of application that hides sexy photos and texts. Not that I would ever have looked through her phone. I'm not that kind of guy.

At this point, I didn't even know if the baby was mine. She'd been having unprotected sex with him. I took a two-month stress leave from work to think about things, and I decided, ultimately, that I couldn't stay with her.

When I got back to work, an oversight on my boss's end cost me what's called a workplace safety violation. I'm a union worker, and I love my job. I remember sitting there with my union rep, feeling like I was about to lose my mind because everything was falling apart and I could potentially lose my job. Until they sorted everything out, which ultimately took six months, I had to show up at work every day and not work. Let me tell you, there's nothing worse than telling a depressed man to just sit with his thoughts for six months.

In the meantime, the board held a hearing on the complaint against my wife, and they told her she would be facing $90,000 in fines and a permanent suspension of her license. I told her to tell them that she was seeking counseling, that she was repentant—to use all the buzzwords to get them to reduce the fines, at least. Ultimately, they suspended her license for five years—after which, to regain the right to practice, she would have to go back to school for another three years—and she was fined $3,500.

There was no way I was going to kick the (possible) mother of my child out on the street, and neither of us could afford to rent, so we ended up living together, as roommates, while the divorce was getting processed. We had no savings: before everything fell apart, we used the little money that we had saved to take a real estate course. We got into the business of buying and selling storage lockers. I had equity on the house, so I contacted a hard-money lender to get that initial seed money. We were so close to turning a profit, until she lost her job. And then the lender refused to finance me anymore and we lost the business.

She didn't work again, obviously, so I paid for everything. I did notice that $600 was showing up in our bank account every month, and I asked her where it came from—turns out, she'd taken out a loan from her father. The money eventually stopped. The poor guy went broke, too. But she and I were very good roommates. I'm a very forgiving and generous person, which I think gave her the wrong impression about where we stood with each other. Since things seemed amicable and we still lived together, she didn't want to believe that it was over. I told her, "I forgive you for cheating on me. But lying to me about the extent of the cheating, making me question the paternity of the baby—that, I feel terrible about. We can't come back from that."

To add to our already stressful living situation, my oldest son from my first marriage has moved in, too. My ex-wife refuses to sign the separation agreement paper stating that he's living with me because she wants to keep getting the child-support payments. She and I were high school sweethearts—we met when she was a freshman and I was a sophomore. She's not a very nice person, but unfortunately I found that out too late. She has no empathy for other people at all. My son called me crying one night because she had threatened to punch him. The poor kid was sleeping with a pellet gun to protect himself. I couldn't have that, so I moved him in with me.

I still have about $80,000 in debt from legal fees from my first divorce, so I have to represent myself in all legal matters, from the most recent divorce to any prior custody and child-support issues, because I can't afford a lawyer. The bank is making a killing off overdraft fees and interest payments on my accounts. On top of that, the court is garnishing my wages for child support; thankfully, I was able to amend the child support order to the proper amount with arrears, but they sent me to collections six months later, claiming that I hadn't been paying enough. It's a mess. My son is still in high school, but he's a good kid; he got a job and he pitches in whatever he can. The only light at the end of the tunnel is that the house value has appreciated in the last few years—it basically doubled in value—and we're putting it on the market in May. My second ex and I should each walk out with a bit of money—enough to make a fresh start or, in my case, just barely get myself out of debt. And if my day job doesn't work out, I could always try my hand at lawyering. I'm basically an expert in family law.

I have a friend who works as a crisis counselor and sometimes he uses me as an example of the guy who always ends up in the eye of the hurricane, in the perfect storm. He tells people who are in trouble: "It can always be worse. Things will turn around."

I've never had it easy—everything I've ever done has been a challenge. I was raised not to complain, though, and I learned from my folks that life can get really hard, but as long as you band together and look at the glass as half full, things always work out.

My friend was right—things did turn around. My son was born in September, and it wasn't until February that we got the results of the cheek swab for the paternity test. It confirmed that the baby is mine. He came out looking like an old man, a wise soul, so I call him "little geezer." He's such a happy baby, and looking at him at any given moment helps me realize how lucky I am. So there's reason to celebrate after all. I guess the lesson here is, no matter what happens, try to laugh about it, and try to look on the bright side. Oh, and don't get divorced.

Erika, early twenties

I look like a normal girl. I have a normal face and normal eyes. I speak like a normal person. During my freshman year of college, I became an escort, and everything stopped being normal.

I felt really alone in college. I went from living at home with my family to having nobody around except for a mismatched roommate. I attended classes and tried to meet people there, but I had a lot of trouble reaching out to my peers in a way that didn't feel awkward or like I was desperate. It felt easier to build relationships online, where anonymity made it seem like I had so much less to lose. So I started reaching out to people, mostly people on dating sites and meet-up groups. That's where I met someone who gave me cocaine for the first time. He took me to a couple of house parties with shady characters. Eventually he introduced me to Mandy, who was supposed to be my hookup. Mandy was a prostitute, but I didn't know that when I first met her.

She was a tall and pretty brunette with really intense green eyes. I called her Cruella de Vil once, and she thought it was funny. She had her clothes tailor-made and she was hypersexual. I was drawn to her voice—she had a kind of crackly smoker's voice, low and sultry—and to the fact that no matter where she was, she never seemed alone. She was always surrounded by people who hung on her every word. She wasn't "normal."

Our relationship went into fast-forward mode. I had known her for a couple of days, but she treated me—everyone, really—with indiscriminate familiarity. I was "babe" or "love"—never Erika. I started to doubt that she knew my name. While her attention was on me, Mandy was very good at making me feel like I was the only person who mattered. I started noticing that I didn't like it when her attention flitted away to someone else. It felt, somehow, like I'd failed to keep her happy. So I started to become addicted to her, to what she offered.

She glamorized her life—she had the hookups for the best clothes, the "in" to the best clubs. When she first took me to her apartment, she had a pile of money on her bed. I was snorting cocaine every day at this point—probably about $100 worth a day, which really isn't that much—and I occasionally took Molly and ketamine. Of course, I was also on painkillers and drinking pretty heavily. At this point, I was using my student loans to buy the drugs, and I was totally broke. So when I saw all that money . . . let's just say I'd kind of already made up my mind. Whatever she was doing, however she was getting that money, I was all in.

I wasn't really Mandy's victim. She just took advantage of what was in front of her. She helped me set up my ads on Backpage and Eros. I charged between $100 and $400, depending on what the clients wanted. When I first started out, I forgot to ask for the money up front once and the guy left without paying me. From then on, once the clients came into the apartment, I'd take the money first and take it away to a different room. Then, I did whatever they paid for.

On the weekends, I made up to $2,000.

At first, I got to keep everything I made. I used all of it for drugs; at my very worst, I was using about $200 worth of cocaine a day, but I was on a lot of other things, too. I started selling sex to pay for the drugs, but then I was on the drugs to keep selling sex—to live through the day and do what I had to do. I always wondered when that switch happened.

About a month or two into us working together, Mandy started coming up with reasons why she needed help with money. First, she needed to see the dentist. Then, she needed a fix for the car. Sometimes she was short on rent. I always helped her; I was naively happy to do it. But eventually, the reasons stopped coming—she just started demanding money. I gave her about half of what I made, sometimes more, sometimes everything. She became, essentially, my pimp.

Over the months, I started getting regulars who wanted to see me once or twice a week. If I count my regulars once, I slept with anywhere from three hundred to five hundred different men in a two-year period. I spent whole weekends with people and got paid lump sums to be totally at their disposal. I made hundreds of thousands of dollars. I have none of it.

Some clients were just lonely. Some guys are into different things that they can't tell their wives and girlfriends about: one wanted me to blow up a bunch of balloons and sit on them. There was something puritan about him. He never asked to have sex with me or to touch me. He never even touched himself. He just put the $120 on the dresser and quietly sat on the bed, watching me in an almost passive way. He wanted me to look right at him, maintaining eye contact as I lowered myself onto a balloon, and then move from one to the other carefully—without bursting any of them—in a room that looked like an explosion of candy buttons.

I didn't mind it at all—the only annoying bit was that I had to blow up the balloons myself, which took me at least half an hour and always left me light-headed. Also, I hated the way that the static made my hair float for hours after I was done. All in all, though, this was the most bearable appointment of my week. I tried to be sexy about the whole thing, but it was just plain weird, even for me. The more I thought about it, though, I would take weird any day over what my other clients asked me to do.

I used to meet one guy in his home and we had sex surrounded by photos of his wife and kids. I refused to do it on the bed. Another guy was into choking. He got off on the sound of me gasping for air, he told me. And the helpless look in my eyes. He also liked to spit on my face. I wouldn't have seen him again, but he paid well: $2,000 a week. After he had choked me out one time, I ran out of the room and was crying on the couch. When I eventually went back, he looked up at me and, politely as can be, asked if he could use my bathroom. I kind of numbly nodded—like, *You almost killed me, but you're asking if you can use my bathroom?*

While all of this was happening, I was still in school. My grades obviously started suffering. I didn't go to class, but I'd show up to take the exams. Having that responsibility kept me grounded in reality—like I couldn't totally drop off the face of the earth because school would notice. But dipping my toe into normalcy also made me feel like even more of an outsider than I had before. The girls in Lululemon, talking about this weekend's frat party, would never have cut it one day in the life I lived. Eventually, I dropped out. My parents were pretty clueless about everything. I think they sensed that something was wrong with me, but they never really asked, you know? And how do you tell your dad about something like this? I just couldn't do it.

Weirdly, what kept me going was my relationship with Mandy. She had me thinking that we shared something, that we were in on this together. She was telling me that we're not like other people—"We can't relate to normal people," she said. "We've got to stick together, you and I."

It was comforting to have her, even if I knew that she was using me. She had a hold on me. I'd known from the very beginning that I was expendable to her, but I stuck with her. It was the whole idea of collective suffering, you know? I remember she pulled a gun on me once during a fight—I don't remember what about—and hit me on the head with it. We were driving to New Jersey during Hurricane Sandy. Imagine! The streets were totally empty. I was bleeding, and she refused to pull over and let me clean the wound. She had this strange detached look to her that night. But even when it got awful, I was constantly trying to convince myself that it wasn't so bad. Whenever one of the other girls who hung around us tried to approach me or help me, I'd always dismiss it: "You don't know what you're talking about."

Eventually, we got caught in a sting. One of the cops who came, I think with the federal human trafficking task force, locked me in my room and raped me while all his buddies were just outside the door. Then, he let me go.

As awful as it was, I saw this as my second chance. I went home one weekend and I told my parents about what had been happening. Their reaction was weirdly calm—they went into crisis-management mode. They helped me get clean. A few months later, I was allowed back to school. My mom and dad come visit me all the time now. I think they're scared that something will happen again. But I don't think so. This all feels like a strange fluke. I don't know how I got there and how I got so deep. I guess I'm just happy it's over.

LOSS

Henry, seventies

In recovery, they tell you that alcoholism is chronic, progressive, and fatal. But it wasn't until she died that this lesson really resonated. Up until the very end, I thought I could cure her. I thought I could save her.

I met my wife at an interoffice softball game on a weekend afternoon. She wasn't a very good player, and I teased her about that a lot. We quickly became inseparable. She was a formidable woman with a sharp tongue and a quick wit. We dated for a couple of years and then got married.

I had reservations about her drinking from the very beginning, but I loved her and ignored the problems. She tried to hide it from me, and I was a willing accomplice. I didn't want to see it. But in retrospect, I knew that she was an alcoholic—I just knew it in my gut. Later, when we were married and it became painfully obvious that she was ill, it became the two of us against the world, putting on a show, pretending everything was fine. But I needed the good in her, so I took the bad with it, too, because I thought I could fix her.

In the early days of our marriage, we traveled together a lot; we took long road trips and made plans for the future. Before we went to bed each night, we would discuss the places we wanted to explore. We hoped to buy a house in New Orleans and eventually retire there.

I tried to make her happy at all costs, thinking that if I gave her everything she'd ever wanted, she wouldn't need to drink anymore. I saw her need to drink as my personal failure as a husband. We paid for world-class rehab facilities—but every trip ended the same way, with an eventual relapse. Maybe she made it a few days, maybe a few months. But she always relapsed. And it only got worse. It started to consume everything.

I felt like a zombie. I didn't have any feelings other than pain. I was grieving for the loss of the life I thought we would have together. I would look at our stack of postcards and feel like our dreams and plans—which had once seemed so real and reachable—had become fantasies. I was an emotional slave to her, and I couldn't see where she ended and I began. When she was happy, I was happy. When she felt sad, I felt sad. We talked about divorce, but I wasn't ready to give up on her.

I spent countless restless nights making sure that she didn't get sick and asphyxiate. I remember all the times she would wake up in the middle of the night to drink in order to keep her body from going into withdrawal. I became obsessed with making her eat. Her body had started rejecting solid food altogether, favoring alcohol. This is when it first hit me that she was suffering from a disease: I realized that her brain considered withdrawal a bigger threat than lack of food. She was quite tall, my wife—around five foot nine. Toward the end of her life, when her disease was at its worst, she weighed only 110 pounds. It changed how I looked at her; I could no longer blame her. It's like blaming someone for having cancer; she couldn't help that she was sick.

Once, we went out to dinner to celebrate our anniversary. I had put so much time and effort into picking out the restaurant and making the arrangements. I was hoping to recapture the early days of our marriage and that feeling of love and wanderlust that we'd once shared. We both ordered food, and she ordered wine, too. She was drinking quickly and was in bad shape by the time the food arrived. Before the server even had a chance to put the food down, she asked him to take it back and put it in a doggie bag. She said she didn't have an appetite. So we sat in silence, and I ate alone. She just drank.

I started going to Al-Anon meetings at first because I wanted to hear stories from family members who had succeeded in getting their loved ones clean. I know now that I went for the wrong reason. I was supposed to go for me, but I went for her. When I told her I was going that first night, she asked if she could go with me. She was drunk, and I was unaware that she might trigger some of the other participants. I hoped they would tell her how to get clean, so I said she could. When we got there and it was my turn to introduce myself, all I could say was "Hi, I'm Henry," and then I broke down crying. She got up and walked out. The next day, she told me she'd decided to check herself into a ninety-day rehab facility.

I can't tell you how hopeful I felt that night. I danced around our living room after she'd gone to sleep, crying tears of happiness and relief. I thought that perhaps we'd had a breakthrough, that since she was the one who had decided to check herself in this time, things would be different. It would stick. I drove her to the airport the next day—she'd picked one on a beach in Florida. I hoped that the reminder of swimming in the ocean, which she loved, would give her something to stay clean for—would give her the boost she needed to thrive on her sobriety.

The ninety days felt unbearably long. I put myself on a diet and stopped drinking, too. I started working out and taking care of my mental health. I did it to mirror the wellness that she was building in rehab. I wanted to be able to keep up with her once she was better. During my thousand-mile drive to pick her up, I felt giddy with excitement. I imagined someone different—fuller-figured, healthy, happy again. I'd planned a scenic ten-night trip home along the ocean, and I played out our adventures in my mind's eye, smiling to myself, pressing down the gas whenever I thought of seeing her.

When I went to the front desk to pick her up, they put me in a waiting room and you'd have thought I was waiting for a life-or-death verdict. She finally came out, and she looked radiant. She gave me a hug, and we made our way to the car. I told her about the trip I'd planned, and she just lit up—she couldn't wait to get there. And she was good; she was really good for about a day or two. But as we started to drive back up the coast, she started souring. Uncharacteristically, she picked fights with me. She insisted I drop her off at the side of the road one time, and I spent about an hour convincing her to get back in. When we got to our hotel for the night, she almost got a separate room. And that's how it started up again. By the time we were back home, she'd mentally relapsed. She'd had a seizure that first night in rehab after refusing withdrawal medication. At this point, it was obvious that it had changed her personality. She was no longer herself. She got mean.

In a few weeks, she was drinking alcoholically again, despite daily AA meetings and an intensive outpatient program. I took it upon myself to detox her. I found something online that suggested starting out the alcoholic at their original dose—which for her was four or five bottles of red wine a day—and then slowly easing them down to none. So the first day I gave her twenty five-ounce glasses at specific times. I would wake her up in the middle of the night and give her the glass of wine like she was taking medication. The next day, I gave her nineteen, and the next eighteen, until she eventually got down to nothing.

She lasted one week.

Because of her repeated relapses, my family had started distancing themselves from me. John, my son from a previous marriage, resented me for ignoring my family. When John's wife gave birth to a baby boy, my first grandchild, they told me that they didn't want my wife around the boy—that she wouldn't be considered his grandmother. I had done my best to keep her addiction a secret, but it seemed that everyone knew. When my wife found out about John's decision to lock her out of the baby's life, she became angrier and more resentful. Detached from her family and mine, she took out her frustration on her only lifeline—me. And I was already buckling under the weight of my double life. I would write letters to advice columns asking for help—but I never sent them.

My wife became increasingly isolated. She often refused to talk to me at all and spent all day crying and drinking in our room. She'd completely lost her zest for life. She had given up. She started writing me Post-it notes and putting them everywhere. Depending on the day she was having, I found anything from small declarations of love or scribbled memories of better days, to painful accusations or running shopping lists. I'd find them on the fridge, in the pantry, in my closet, in my gym bag, inside my shoes . . . everywhere. And that's how we communicated.

One night, I was getting ready for bed when I heard a crash from the living room. She had fallen and hurt her shoulder. We went to the emergency room, where the doctors informed me that both her blood oxygen and blood pressure were very low. After rehydrating her by early the next morning, the doctors decided to discharge her. When we got home, she ate and wanted to rest. I went to an Al-Anon meeting and got back a couple of hours later. She had been on the phone with her friends and family.

"I've been making amends," she told me with a smile. We sat down on our porch, and we talked about things—about life and her illness. She seemed like her old self. I was very emotional because she was so lucid and present, and the conversation was no longer about if she was sick—we'd both finally acknowledged that—it was about how to get her better.

She told me she was too tired to walk, so I put her in a rolling chair and pushed her to the bedroom. Then she asked me to help her into our bed. I started turning down the bed, and when I turned around she was breathing erratically and she had passed out. I gave her mouth-to-mouth and called the ambulance. When I got to the hospital, the doctors told me it didn't look good. They put her on life support, and she passed away the next morning.

It happened so quickly, and strangely enough, although her death was years in the making, I still wasn't ready for it. I wasn't prepared.

So who am I now? For so many years, my existence was tied to hers. I was her caretaker, and that was the predominant part of my identity. And when she died, I lost myself. I spent days in my house, in my bathrobe, depressed. I still do. It's been almost a year, and I'm struggling to do even the most basic things—to settle her estate, to execute her will, to sell or donate her things. There are days when I can barely get out of bed—just totally wasted days. I have so little structure left that it's easy to just spiral down into depression.

Her loss has been a gradual unveiling. I still can't talk to anyone who doesn't know what has happened. It's too much pressure—you know?—to act normal when you're grieving. I just can't do it. I can't pretend that my whole world hasn't fallen apart.

But she's everywhere, still. I recently had to go through the bottles she used to carry water (alcohol?) to work—I threw out or donated scores of reusable water bottles. After she died, I was standing in front of the closet, trying to pick out a jacket to go someplace. I'm not a formal-wear guy, you know. I prefer jeans and a button-down. As I slid my hand in the sleeve to put the jacket on, I felt the faint crumple of some paper, and then I saw a Post-it zigzag to the floor. I almost didn't want to look at it. I was afraid it would be an unpleasant reminder.

It said, *I love you.*

Patrick, late forties

I come from a very conservative Episcopalian family, the youngest of four raised in a small town in New Hampshire. My parents were tough, distant. We were well-off so I never went without, but we didn't hug or tell each other "I love you." I guess, in that sense, I did go without. We were raised with discipline and the pursuit of excellence in our blood. The problem was, I didn't know where I fit in in the world. I craved belonging. When I saw a Marines recruitment poster one day, that was it. I was in.

I graduated from USMC recruit training in June 1990. I was twenty years old. They sent me overseas from August 1990 to June 1991 for the Gulf War. I was stationed on the USS *Tripoli*, which was hit by a mine. Then I was stationed on the ground in Okinawa for six months, then in Mogadishu. I was there for the Battle of Mogadishu. Before I was stationed there, I didn't even know where Somalia was.

Mogadishu was the beginning of the end for me. A part of me died there. I lost my religion. I believed that if there was a God, this place would not exist. Our main reason for being there was to help the UN bring food to the people—people dying of starvation. There were bodies all over the place, little kids, man. Babies. I joined the Marines to get out of New Hampshire, to see the world. But seeing the way that people lived there ignited such a dissonance in me, such internal turmoil. I always knew that I came from money. We had a nice house, food on the table, a place to sleep. We lived in the best country in the world. Somalia, on the other hand, wasn't far off from those infomercials that try to get you to donate money to a child in need—distended bellies, naked babies, no food, no water. I'd had a blessed life that I really hadn't appreciated.

We got embroiled in the worst US battle since Vietnam. Aidid, the warlord responsible for the death of his people, told Somalis that we were there to convert them to Christianity. So they fought us hard. I am not a violent person, but people conform to their environment. Shooting a gun, when I think back on it, was a very surreal experience. I was more afraid of shooting someone than I was of getting shot. People who have seen combat understand this. I was afraid that killing would break something, rewire me or something. And it really does—something changes, forever.

I stayed in the Marines for another few years. In 1994, I was twenty-four. I had come home from combat to being a civilian in the real world. I had nothing. Well, that's not true. I had PTSD, and I was scared for the first time. My roommate told me that I was yelling and talking in my sleep. What you have to do when you're overseas is so instilled in you that you never think about it. But when you come back, you have all the time in the world, so you get to thinking and dreaming. And pretty soon, you can't get away from what you've seen and what you've done. I was living in Arlington, Virginia, when I tried cocaine for the first time. And I realized, "I don't ever want to *not* feel like this again."

A couple of years later, one of my sisters decided to move to Chicago, and I followed her there. We'd always been close, and I needed someone who cared for me—someone important to keep me around; plus, there was nothing left for me in Virginia. In Chicago, I was bouncing at a nightclub and doing coke very casually, on and off. When I met Maria at the club one night, it was a second chance at it all. My responsibility to her kept me sane. We became great friends first, and then we started dating and got engaged about two and a half years in. While we were engaged, she got pregnant. Her father was Irish Catholic and very religious, but a shotgun wedding was out of the question—the timing wouldn't have worked—so her mother convinced her to get an abortion. After that, the relationship fizzled.

It was a difficult breakup. Not nasty, just protracted. She battled depression for eight months after the abortion and was very codependent. Her parents supported her. One day, I just packed up and left. I couldn't do it anymore. It was too dark—between my own issues, our loss, her depression, I was starting to feel like it was getting to be too much to handle without losing my mind. I just needed to go, to detach.

I googled her about a year ago and found out that her dad died. I almost sent flowers, and I've wanted to write, many times, to apologize for walking away. She's the only person I've ever loved. If I could do it over again, I would have stayed.

I'd been involved with a woman once before I met Maria, in between the Gulf and Somalia. Samantha was in an abusive relationship and she left him for me. She got pregnant. When I got deployed to Somalia, she went back to her ex, who was a violent dude. Our little boy, Ben, died of SIDS when he was four months old. I found out when I got back. Jill, the girl who'd introduced me to Sam, told me about what had happened—that they had investigated but couldn't prove anything. I thought about reaching out to Sam, but it was easier to just walk away. I don't know if I walked away because I never wanted a kid to begin with, so letting go was easy, or because I was afraid of what would happen to her if her ex found out that the baby wasn't his.

After leaving Maria, I supported myself with odd jobs and stayed mostly clean. In the early 2000s, things fell apart. My mother was diagnosed with cancer and died soon after. I was in NYC when the planes hit the towers—I was actually in the lobby of the second building. I think the emotional weight of my mother's diagnosis, along with the close call in New York, sent me over the edge and I started using again. At the time, I was working as a headhunter for a health-care company, but they fired me because of my cocaine issue and gave me six months' salary as part of the severance package.

The package was a good chunk of money, so I didn't leave my apartment for weeks. I started out at about half an ounce and worked my way up to an ounce and a half of cocaine a week. I just sat on my couch, watching TV footage of kids being sent abroad for the Second Gulf War and the fear and rage resurfaced, but multiplied threefold—worse than I've ever experienced. I was in tears, shaking, afraid of what the soldiers would have to come back to, angry for them.

Getting high meant having a chance to detach from everything that happened, or at least to put a little distance between myself and the memories. With every hit I took—the abortion, Ben dying, my mom dying, 9/11—I floated a little further and further away. And eventually I realized I just didn't really want to come back.

I went on a pretty bad binge one day, and I was feeling really ill, so I decided that I was going to try to sweat it out. I filled my tub up with hot water. I lowered myself into it, and I swear it felt like I was having a heart attack. I got tunnel vision, I couldn't breathe, and my chest felt tight. I crawled out of the tub and dragged myself on the floor to the corded phone in my living room. I called my sister and I told her, "I think I'm dying." And I wasn't afraid at all. It's just that I'd seen the pain my father went through when my mother died, and I was apprehensive about his ability to survive me. My brother-in-law called an ambulance, and I made it through, but my addiction just got worse. I disappeared for months and went on weeklong cocaine binges. I was afraid to sleep because of the nightmares. My poor sister was losing her mind with worry.

After a couple of months of trying to track me down, she finally found an address for me and called the police to do a wellness check. They approached the apartment and noted that there was a smell coming from inside. They communicated as much to her, assuming that what they were smelling was my decomposing body. When they finally got the keys to the door and entered the apartment, they saw my fish tank in a state of complete decay. After that, my sister insisted that I move to Florida so that she could keep an eye on me, but I pulled even further away. I ended up in California for a job, living like I had a death wish. I got myself arrested on purpose, because behind bars was the only place I felt safe from myself. I called my sister—it was actually her birthday that day, what a present—and she sent a lawyer to bail me out.

My dad picked me up at the airport once I flew back to the East Coast. He took me to a dual diagnosis-rehab center in a swanky facility. They diagnosed me with bipolar disorder and said that the PTSD was the underlying cause of my addiction. That was the first of three rehab stints that my father paid for. Every cent was a loan that I've had to pay back, and he didn't let me forget it.

Ultimately, I am lucky. I have a family that cares about me enough to check in and worry when they haven't heard from me in a while. I'm sure I would have died many times if I didn't have them tethering me to this world. I care too much about them to inflict that kind of pain on them. And my life hasn't all been a total wash: I started a couple of successful companies (sold one, lost the other) and was making very good money for a while. And I'm pretty certain I can get back to that space—where productivity feels good and I have a little more perspective on my life.

Between my son's death, my mom's death, the abortion, four Marine buddies who committed suicide after coming home, and the nightmares from my own days of combat, I sure have got a lot to run from. Addiction feels a little bit like being stuck in a hamster wheel.

The other day, I finally came up with a good way to explain addiction: I went to wash a dish and when I turned the faucet on, scalding-hot water came out. For the first split second that my hand was in the water, though, it was hard to tell if it was really cold water or really hot water. It takes a second, a peaceful, painless second, for your body and brain to process what's happening to it. And I realized that for me, that's the draw of cocaine—that first split second after doing a line when you don't know yet if you're really living or finally dying.

Louise, fifty

Tomorrow is the nine-year anniversary of my Will's death. Before this weekend's over, I'm going to sit somewhere and scream and cry and ask why and what if, even though I know better. And I'll say, *If only*, too. And then I'll put my grief away and move on with my life until next August 5. Because I have to. People don't know how to deal with that kind of grief—the grief of a parent who has lost a child. They say things like "God had a plan," and "It was his time to go." I've been guilty of saying things like that, too. People just don't know better. And I don't want them to know better. I want them to be spared having to know firsthand.

I was seven months pregnant with Will when I went into premature labor. He was born three pounds and three ounces, and they told me he wouldn't live. His lungs were filling with blood because his heart wasn't fully developed. They told me that, to give him the slightest chance of survival, they needed to operate—open-heart surgery on a three-pound newborn. But first they wanted to try an experimental drug, a synthetic version of a hormone produced by eight-month-pregnant women that might close the hole in his heart. We gave them the okay, and they gave him the first dose and scheduled the open-heart surgery, just in case. The odds weren't good: they gave Will a 10 percent chance of survival.

When they finally tested his heart after three doses of the drug, they saw that the hole was 100 percent closed. They tested his hearing, too: perfect. His eyesight: perfect. He came home with us a week later. The only long-term effect was that, because of the breathing tubes, Will always spoke with a slight lisp.

He grew up to be so full of life. The youngest of my four kids, he was also my only son. He was the class clown. Girls in middle school run in packs like wild dogs. At any given time, there would be ten of my daughters' girlfriends in my house, and they all treated him like their little brother. He loved it. He was the most popular kid in school because he was so close to them. I used to tell Will, "You're either going to grow up being one of the few men in this world who truly understands women, or you're going to be gay. And I'm okay with either."

Will didn't have an easy childhood—none of my kids did. I dated John, the guy who first got me pregnant, from the time I was thirteen to when I turned seventeen. I got pregnant the first time we had sex, go figure. He got himself in trouble with the law and they locked him up. I walked away. I didn't want anything to do with that type of lifestyle, and I raised my kids with the mind-set that if they ever ended up in trouble, call me, but don't think I'm going to come bail you out. I'm still here; I still got your back. If you're falling, I'm here to catch you. But I want to know what branches you tried to reach for on your way down. I want to know that you tried to help yourself.

I met Paul through a friend of John's. Paul asked me out. I was a single teenaged mom. The baby needed a dad. So I did what I needed to do and I married him three weeks later. I walked that line of moving from place to place and living paycheck to paycheck and having another three kids, and I realized that the person I was most disappointed in was myself. But I stuck with my marriage, even when things got bad. I wasn't a child of divorce. I didn't believe in it. I'm kind of stubborn, I guess you could say.

After a few years, Paul started losing his mind. He put my photo on his jacket and on keychains. He'd sit out in the parking lot while I was at work, and when he thought I was being too flirtatious, he would become violent. He was deteriorating mentally, and I didn't realize that. I mean, he was always a wild card, and when things were good, they were great. But when they were bad, they were really bad.

I remember one time he gave me a black eye because I bought

a tube of hamburger meat to make for dinner that was "too fatty." I hit him over the head with a frying pan. Eventually, though, I got tired of fighting back and started thinking maybe it would end faster if I didn't resist. I left Paul when Will was three because I didn't want my son to grow up to be that kind of man, and I didn't want my daughters to think this was an okay way to be treated. I filed for divorce and was granted emergency custody until it could be finalized.

Paul came and took the kids one day. He dropped the girls off at their grandmother's and he took off with Will. He was gone for days and wouldn't give me my son back until I agreed to go back to him. I told him I would, but only if he let me go back to school and get my GED so that I could help him with bills. He kept his word. I went back, got my GED, and even went back to complete higher education, and I got a better job, too. He was at work the day I moved out—I took my kids and left. I bought a single-wide trailer with the money I had saved and stuck it out on my granddaddy's land in the country.

Paul told me that he was willing to go to counseling to keep the family together. I went to the hospital with him to see if we could get him admitted because he wasn't well emotionally. The social worker talked to him for a little while, and then she came to talk to me. This woman told *me*, a victim of domestic violence, that I needed to give him a second chance. So I did. He never raised his hand, hollered, or talked back to me ever again. He was doing everything he could to make the little trailer I bought nicer for us. He was trying to make it a home. But it was gone for me. I couldn't let him back into my life, my bed. I told him, "You've hurt me more than I love you."

One night, after I went to school, he put the kids to bed, and he hung himself. He was twenty-nine years old. I found him. He had a suit on the bed—I'm assuming he put it out because it was the one he wanted to be buried in. I tried to get him loose but couldn't. I ran down to my mama's and I busted the window in the front door to get to the phone. I called the police, and then I went back to the bedroom to get him down again, but it already seemed too late. They called it a passive hanging because he took the rope and tied it to a piece of wood on the ceiling, got on his knees, and leaned into it.

He left a note. The last line read, "When I said 'til death do us part,' I meant it."

Luckily, the kids slept through it all. When they woke up, they assumed there was a car wreck. I let them believe it for three days until I had some time to sit down and explain what had happened to each one of them, to the extent that they could understand.

I spent the next five years on my own, fixing all the things that were wrong with me, that had led me to the situation I was in. I fixed the things that made me weak and made it so that I couldn't be so easily exploited by someone. And when Dave, an old friend, asked me to marry him for the second time, I wizened up and told him yes. He wore me down. He's been my best friend for twenty-seven years. We started dating in February, and I married him in March. You'd think I would have learned to not marry someone so soon. But this time it was right. I married someone who, instead of planting me to the ground, gave me wings. He's the light at the end of the tunnel. And he was an amazing father to my children.

So . . . Will. I guess I've been avoiding talking about the day he died.

He poked his head into my room and told me he was going to run to the store to get some snacks. I was lying down reading. I hadn't been feeling good. He asked if I wanted anything from the store, and I told him no and that I had a bad case of the blues. He said, "I love you," and he left. I went to the laundry room to get a load done, and then I thought to ask him to get a Diet Coke. I followed him out and I saw him by his car, and I could hear him and Dave laughing. And I said to myself, *Never mind, I won't interrupt them.* So I saw him get in his car, and I waved to him as he drove off.

A woman was stopped in the left lane, and she didn't have her blinker on. To keep from hitting her, Will had swerved and overcorrected. He went into oncoming traffic. The car flipped three times and the airbag didn't deploy. He hit his head against the driver's window, and the seat belt cut off his oxygen. They medevaced him, but between the loss of oxygen (he went without for eleven minutes), and hitting his head on the window, they weren't sure what caused him to be brain-dead.

August 5 was a Wednesday. At the hospital, I would not let them declare him dead. Although he was brain-dead, the only thing that was wrong with him when you looked at him was the bruise from the seat belt. You couldn't even tell that he'd been in a wreck. I made them do testing. Flashlight in the eye. Needle in the feet. I watched it. I wanted to make sure that there was no reaction. And there was none.

So they got the trauma team ready and notified the organ transplant people. Will had wanted to be an organ donor because Dave has kidney issues and is on a transplant list. They sent in a rep to talk to us and kept him alive until the recipients could be gathered. On Friday morning, they took him down to harvest his organs and we finally left the hospital. We never left his side from the time of the wreck until he went in for the surgery. I couldn't leave him. I was there from his very first heartbeat until his last.

What was so amazing about this child was that when I had him, I was in a bad marriage and in a bad place, twenty years old, three other kids. I thought long and hard about an abortion. And I couldn't do it. When he was born like he was, with all the things that were wrong with him, I prayed to God I'd done the right thing. And to this day, nine years after his death, there has been no rejection of his organs. Every single organ he donated is alive.

I'm in touch with one of the recipients. His name is Tim, and he is from Mississippi. He got one of Will's kidneys. He is an amazingly nice person. Tim got to meet his grandson because of Will. Every year at Christmastime, we decorate our tree and we call it

Will's tree. And every year, like clockwork, Tim sends me a Christmas ornament. And I buy a special ornament, too, so I can still get a gift for my child.

Will's liver went to a Cantonese lady in Atlanta—she wrote me a letter. His heart is with an RN from North Carolina. His lung is in a Vietnam vet. His other kidney went to a little boy named Eli, who was born with medical problems, so his mom put him in foster care. The lady who wrote me about Eli told me that after he got a kidney and started getting better, he got adopted, and today is a perfect and happy little boy. She sent me a picture of him—and he's posing in this strange position with his feet spread and his arms up in the air. I have a photo of Will in the same exact pose. Who knows what this little boy will go on to accomplish. His story changed because he got Will's kidney.

The parts of my son that are still here, the parts that I felt grow in my tummy, have got no quit. The heart they said was never going to work is still going; the lungs are still going. And I got to be a part of that amazing story. As long as there's a part of him in this world, his story continues.

Aaron, fifties

That first moment of wakefulness in the hospital, I will always remember with dread. I opened my left eye first; my right one held out, rooted down and refusing to see the astringent room. As soon as my body awoke, I felt a sharp pain and braced as it spread through me like a sea of fire. It slowly started dawning on me—where I was, and why—but before I could think, I pumped my PCA, a little button that sent anesthetics into my bloodstream, and felt my body relax back into the bed. The white sheets enveloped me, and I drifted to sleep.

I couldn't have been out for longer than a few hours when I heard muffled voices over the distinctive sound of the wound vac. Of all the unpleasantness of war and its side effects, my least favorite was the wound vac: a vacuum cleaner that sucks dead tissue from the wound in order to promote healing. They had come around to clean out what was left of my right leg—they amputated it below the knee and took half of my left foot—and I kept my eyes shut even though I was wide awake and in full panic. The stench of rotting flesh traveled up to my nose, and I was instinctively ashamed that my body had produced such a smell. It all came back to me in an instant: the explosion, the dull static in my ears, and then nothingness. In the past week, I'd been on Vicodin, morphine, and Dilaudid, but no cocktail of narcotics took away the dull ache that I felt in both my legs. I wasn't sure anymore if I was imagining it, or if it had always felt like that. I pumped my PCA again.

Over the next few months, when I did the balance exercises during physical therapy, there'd be moments that I'd forget what had happened. I'd walk around the cones my therapist had set up on the floor, and for a second I'd feel my fleshy feet hit the ground as they always did, when I was young, when I played sports, when I was normal and whole, before the war. But when I looked down, I saw the metal contraptions that had replaced much of my legs. I would chuckle to myself because I immediately felt wobbly again and went back to feeling as if I were walking on stilts. The brain can play cruel tricks.

I was alone a lot, but not really. I was in the VA, and I went to a military amputee clinic, too, so I was surrounded by people who had been through war and lost a part of themselves, just like I had. But we were all in our own little worlds. People injured in war don't want to be reminded; they don't want to talk about it. They just want to move on. But they all have that look—they look intently at the nothingness in front of their eyes, their brains probably projecting some horror that only they had seen. At night, they'd jump and scream and wake up sweating and crying for their mothers. It was like we were children again.

After almost two years, they let me go home. My wife awkwardly helped me into the back of the van, and I thought I smelled booze on her. She had changed while I was gone—her eyes seemed sunken deeper into their sockets, her hands seemed colder, and she went rigid every time I touched her. I knew she was drinking again, and I knew she was seeing other men. Her excuses, her erratic "work schedule"—none of it made sense. Plus, I could just sense it.

The drive home was excruciating—I sweat through my shirt and dug my nails into the palms of my hands until they both bled. Every slight honk, every sudden stop, every churn of the engine would bring me back to that day, that exact moment, when our vehicle was blown feet into the air—and then minutes afterward, when I awoke.

I tried shutting it out—tried telling myself that I wasn't there anymore, that I was safe, and that I was finally home. But home was so different from how I had imagined it when I was away. I'd imagined warm yellows and soft pinks. I'd imagined the sunlight seeping through our kitchen blinds. I'd imagined my daughters and my wife—their voices ricocheting sweetly through the house like a wind chime.

But everything was gray. When I shut my eyes, I couldn't stop the landscape of the barren desert from projecting itself inside my head and into my mind's eye. I couldn't stop the ringing in my ears. I couldn't stop the images in my head from popping up over and over again, like a broken video game.

"Well, I've settled your stuff in the basement," she said when we got home. I instinctively knew that she wanted me out of the way, that the simple sight of me disturbed her, disgusted her, and frightened her. I was the fly in her ointment. I knew because I'd felt the same way about myself for two years: that the sight of me was enough to ruin anyone's day.

That's kind of how it happens—how veterans end up forgotten, underserved, or homeless. Our mental struggles aren't understood well. We have trouble adjusting when we're back. Our families, through no fault of their own, don't get what we've been through. There's a gap between how things were and how things are, and not a lot of people know how to bridge it, how to make it okay. So we're pushed aside. We're not prioritized. And we internalize that; we learn how to get out of the way, how to stop being inconvenient. It feels like we've given what was needed and now, well, now we're not needed anymore. We're on our own. And that's a hard pill to swallow.

"You'll have some stairs to climb in the morning but that oughta help you with your exercises," she said over her shoulder as she reached into the freezer for the handle of vodka.

I remember making my way down the stairs wordlessly and collapsing onto the gray couch, surveying the room. Odd remnants of my years of service—spare uniforms and boots, my bag, a blanket— were all crumpled up in the corner of the room next to a portable fridge. They looked so insignificant, so unimpressive—the sum of it all, right there. No respect. I had this weird feeling of loss, like I was mourning someone. Except I didn't know who.

It snuck up on me—that feeling of not being whole anymore, not equal, of being less than a man. This homecoming was heartbreaking, and I wondered if I'd have been better off dead. That tiny basement room closed in on me then. I looked down at my legs and cried for the first time. While I was in the hospital and in recovery, I'd kept telling myself that things would turn around once I was home. But seeing what home had become broke my heart. It felt like a final loss of hope.

I wouldn't really say that I'm over it yet, although it's been a few years, but I guess I'm through the worst of it. I've tried dealing with it through prayer, therapy, and humor. Sometimes they work, sometimes not. It's obvious that I'm a military amputee, so when people ask me what happened—and to be fair, they seldom do—I just tell them that they fell off and I'm waiting for them to grow back. Because nobody really wants to hear the truth.

Through cognitive behavioral therapy, I've learned what to do when the thoughts begin to spiral. I can notice when I'm about to go down the rabbit hole, and most times, I can stop myself. But when I can't, I know it's going to be a dark few days. I don't struggle with PTSD anymore so I can do things—like driving without having to worry that I'll get triggered. That's a big part of my recovery, and I'm lucky because it seems that I haven't had it as rough as most guys I know. Mostly, therapy has helped me not be angry anymore. I used to feel that I had given up so much—for what? For what? For what? But I've stopped asking. All I need to know is that it happened, and I've made my peace with it. A lot of people I served with feel that they were wronged, cheated. It is what it is.

I read the Bible and self-help books. I listen to Joel Osteen. Sometimes I call into Prayerline to talk to other people and tell them how I'm feeling, if I'm particularly low. I go to church a lot. Really, I do anything that helps me feel less alone. What has hurt most since coming home has been not feeling loved. Back when I was in a wheelchair, and then in a walker, and then on crutches, I used to fall down a lot. My wife would just stand there and watch me struggle on the floor. She never helped. When she'd been drinking and I'd fall, she'd laugh at me.

It's difficult. I feel partly responsible for what has happened to our marriage. The distance was hard on us. The injuries, even harder. It can't have been simple to raise our daughters alone when I was away. I'm not trying to blame her. But I guess my sacrifice would seem more bearable if it felt appreciated by someone. And not in a "Thank you for your service" type of way. But really. It hurt to see my things in the basement. It hurt. I thought I was coming home to a family, but pieces of us got lost along the way, too.

I'm not sure what will become of us. On my part, I'd like to wait until our youngest goes off to college and then I'll give my wife a divorce if she wants it. My daughters keep me going. They're a big bright spot in my life, and I just don't want their lives to be disrupted by this. They've been through enough.

When I was overseas—I served two tours, and I was in Afghanistan for a total of eighteen months—I'd think about why I was there. When all you see around you is war and destruction and people dying, you do a lot of deep thinking. The mercenary nature of being a soldier can make the killing feel impersonal, so I needed to hold on to something so that I could hold on to my humanity. I needed a way to ground myself so that I didn't lose my mind out there. And I always held on to my family and my home, the way that I imagined them: my wife and our daughters in the backyard with the sun shining on them.

Damon, fifties

Once, a very long time ago, I had a good job, a loving family, and a white picket fence. I started my own business, worked hard, and collected the toys that the wealthy have—a boat, a mansion, a few Harleys. I worried about the things you probably worry about—the stress of work every Monday morning, the bills that kept piling up, and the fact that the more we had, the more it didn't quite seem like enough.

Then, following the financial crisis in 2007–2008, I lost my business, my family, and my home. I lost everything.

You know what they say: when it rains, it pours. The same week that our business went under, my wife's younger sister, Sarah, was killed in a tragic car accident. She was dating a naval cadet who was set to graduate the next day. They were on their way back from the ball before graduation when he lost control of the car and crashed. Sarah died in the wreck. He was able to get to the highway to flag down help, but he was struck and killed instantly. I was depressed, and we needed money and a car; I was looking for a job, any job, to pay off our bills and debt. I worked anything I could get my hands on—lawn care, mechanic, pawnshop—and drove a dead woman's car around all day.

After months of trying to dig myself out of a financial hole, I gave up and started making some very bad decisions. For one, I started sleeping with my landlord. She was married, and her husband was a cop. But she was attractive, and she made herself very available, so it was easy to make irrational choices. The first time, she asked me to help her move some things into her beach house. She came on to me—she was very aggressive—and I didn't resist. She wanted to leave the window open so that people could watch us. I let her do whatever she wanted. She was exciting and made me feel alive, and for those few hours that we were together, I wasn't focusing on my problems. After fourteen years of sobriety, she got me drinking again. We started going to bars every night. Twice, I rode the Harley to Key West and, another time, to Bourbon Street in New Orleans—drunk and high. My wife found out eventually, of course, and she left me.

I don't blame her. Things got really hard for us, and I wasn't a partner to her. I didn't deal with it well. We needed a steady hand at the helm, and I was out cavorting. I thought it was situational depression, but the doctors diagnosed me with bipolar disorder, too, and put me on medication. I was very active and social during this time, but I also felt dulled, lethargic, and sleepy. What they say is right: on the medication, the lows don't feel so low, but the highs don't feel quite as high, either. It was like draining the color out of a painting: the essence is still there and perhaps it's still beautiful, but the playfulness—the joy—is gone. So I got off the meds and let myself feel everything. Life was definitely broken.

At my lowest, I was certain there was only one way out. I wanted one permanent, final solution. My uncle had done it years before. We worked together for fifteen years and we were very close. He retired, and I thought things were going well for him—we even talked about buying investment properties together. About a month after he retired, I received a phone call that he had committed suicide. The way he did it was horrific. He drove to a remote area, got into the back seat of his vehicle, placed two five-gallon cans of gas next to him, and lit them on fire. The explosion was very big. I visited the site and there were car parts scattered everywhere. They told me that there wasn't very much of him left to identify. What a way to go.

It was Halloween night, and I was drunk. And as I swiped the rope like a rosary through my fingers, I thought about my wife or kids being called to the scene to identify me. I thought about the person who would discover me hanging from some tree, and about how maybe that would mess them up, too. I thought about the permanence of the decision—*am I thinking clearly?* I'd come back to it time and again, for months. The draw of suicide didn't seem like something that would just . . . go away. I'd decided on hanging because it was a sure thing. Many years before, in better times, I'd read about this artist who had committed suicide by taking pills and slashing his wrists—or was it taking pills and shooting himself? Anyways, the point was that he wasn't messing around—this wasn't a call for help—he definitely wanted out. And it's strange that the story of this guy's suicide always stayed with me—something about it left such an impression, almost like my mind was bookmarking it because maybe I knew that someday I'd meet a similar fate. There's no time for second thoughts once that noose is tight on the neck. But I had made up my mind. I wanted out, too.

I'd spent a few hours that day poring over my financial records. What the market crash hadn't taken, I had spent on booze and weed and women. The only thing left was my life insurance policy, which fortunately for my family was pretty hefty. I read the fine print a million times: if I committed suicide, my family would still get the money as long as the policy was taken out more than three years ago. I looked at the date of the policy again, and again, and again, and again.

As soon as I'd confirm that I'd taken it out in August 2003, I'd panic and go back to check. I even thought about asking a lawyer to look the suicide clause over but was afraid of setting off a red flag. I just kept thinking that it would be a shame to kill myself and then have my family not get any money just on a technicality. Then my life would really have been pointless.

I played with the rope some more and looked around the empty parking lot of a shopping center. There was a patch of woods in the back of the lot, and I planned on finding a sturdy tree. I'd packed on some weight in the last few years. I thought about the insurance policy again and had to exercise some restraint to not go back to the office and check the dates one last time. Then, I reached into the back seat and grabbed my stool, opened the car door, and walked toward the woods.

That moment of decision will always stand out to me as one of my clearest, most crystallized memories. I felt no fear at all; on the contrary, I walked with a sense of hope. It was the first time I had thought of the future without feeling doomed. But I also knew myself well enough to know that I was a fickle man in life—a man filled with doubts and weaknesses, and that I needed to do this quickly. Even though I was resolute, I still feared that something would change my mind.

I wanted to be somewhere in the middle of the woods—not so close to the lot that people would see me immediately, but also not so far back that it would take a while to discover my body. I didn't want to stink the place up, and I didn't want animals to find me first. I walked for about a minute, and then took out my phone and activated the flashlight feature.

I felt oddly calm, and I studied the trees with a matter-of-factness. It didn't take me long to find the perfect branch and tie the knot I'd looked up on a YouTube tutorial. In the office, I'd spent about an hour practicing the knot because I read that hanging yourself was a tricky business. If done incorrectly, it could result in some serious pain. And I didn't want to feel pain anymore.

I stood on the stool and put the rope around my own neck. Then I fiddled on my phone to deactivate the flashlight. I didn't want people to see it through the woods and interrupt me before I was done.

As I held the phone, the screen lit up and my daughter's name flashed across, pulsating in the darkness. I started crying in the sort of inconsolable way I'd never let my family see, and then, when I'd composed myself and sobered up enough, I called 911 and checked myself into a psychiatric hospital. They gave me Seroquel to calm me down, and I woke up the next morning in a fog. I thought, *How in the hell did I get here, in a nuthouse on Halloween?* I tried to leave, but they told me that you can't leave once you check yourself in. It's like that "Hotel California" song.

My daughter saved my life that night. I've never told her.

My wife and I are back together. We go to therapy and are working on our marriage. For the most part, we are happy. She has very little sex drive—that's the only thing that is lacking. She only does it because she knows that I need it. During the time that we were separated and I was working on myself, we started "dating" each other again. That's the best sex we've ever had. Sometimes I wish we could go back to that, but then I think of the stability we have now, and I can do without the crazy sex. It's interesting how your perspective changes.

We moved to a different state, far away from the people I used to know, and started over. I'm really ashamed of how I felt and what I got so close to doing, so it's hard to face people. My friends all have their own troubles, I'm sure. But you just don't talk about these things. It's easier to start over where nobody knows your past. I don't think about suicide anymore, just how close I got to it.

We bought a nice Cape Cod—it's just enough space for the two of us—no luxuries, and that's okay. I talk to my daughters every day. I work a nine-to-five. I had my private pilot's license for a few years, I took up skydiving, and I became a fourth-degree Knight of Columbus. In my spare time, I make art—little personalized tchotchkes for people. I sell them on Etsy. And I gotta tell you, I'm happy. Happier than I've ever been. Life sure is strange.

Kate, forties

For as long as I can remember, I've slept hard. I always chalked it up to having a physical day job. I work construction in one-hundred-degree weather; that's a man's job if there ever was one. So I figured being extra tired was just part of who I am. When I had my first baby, I told the nurse not to hand him to me.

"But the baby needs to bond," she said, perplexed. "Don't worry, your maternal instinct will kick right in." I insisted: *no*. "My sleep instinct is stronger."

I remember parts of the day it happened. My breast milk was leaking, and the wetness of my shirt must have woken me up. I remember going to get a diaper. He was on the bed in between my legs, and when I went to change him, I noticed that his lips were blue. They could have been blue before that; I don't know. He wasn't breathing. I called 911, then I went back to him and did CPR. When the firefighters came, it didn't seem like they'd been rushing. I guess they thought that the baby was already dead. I remember that they were looking for a baggie for his oxygen, but they didn't have infant sizes. I remember the wallpaper in our kitchen, and the faces of the firefighters as they worked on his tiny little body on the kitchen table. They got a pulse in his leg, and I remember the little sticky EKG pads on it, almost larger than the leg itself. They were there for an hour, and it was touch-and-go. As they left, the firefighters apologized that they couldn't save my son. They said that he died of SIDS. My son was seven days old.

The coroner's report said that he died of "asphyxiation due to overlay." I had always thought that it was SIDS, because that's what the firefighters told me. But then, I never read my son's death certificate until I got in trouble. When the coroner was called in as an expert witness, he said that in his opinion, I had done nothing to purposefully harm the baby.

"It's a matter of opinion," they said, about the decision to change the cause of death.

It took a while, but I moved on with my life, broken as could be. I started dating someone. I wasn't planning on having another kid, not so soon. But I got pregnant, and when she was born, we named her Mary. I was scared of being a mother to Mary, especially after what had happened with my son. I didn't want to be alone with her. She seemed so little and fragile. I also got pregnant with my third very soon after we had Mary—Irish twins, as they call them. I figured, might as well get it over with and have them close in age.

It was night, I guess maybe seven or eight. I fed her, changed her, and swaddled her, and we were on the bed together. I was talking to her and playing with her, and I was wide awake. Ronnie, my boyfriend at the time, came to bed at one point, and then he got back up to do laundry. I guess the movement of the bed must have rolled her closer to me. We had been in the same position for hours when I woke up, again, from my breast milk leaking into my shirt.

Ronnie was in the front room, watching *Survivor*. "I thought about moving you, but you both looked so peaceful," he told me later. I had told him to make sure that I was not alone with the baby, to make sure that I didn't fall asleep holding her. I'd said, "She'll end up on the floor, and I'll know nothing of it." I had told him what had happened with my son, so he should have known better. I should have known better. But it seemed like I couldn't control when I went to sleep—like there was no intervening period of sleepiness or tiredness at all. I'd realize that I'd fallen asleep only once I woke up.

After Mary died, I moved in with my mother, who lived in a different state. I tried to focus on raising my daughter Jamie. I was honest with my doctor right after Jamie was born; I told him that I needed help and that I was having issues with my sleep. Apparently, I don't have a maternal instinct. Instead of helping me, he called

CPS, who called the detectives in my home state, who called CPS back and told them that I was a baby killer. So CPS showed up at my door, and there was a cop with them. They stormed into the house and searched it for Jamie: "Where is the baby? We have to see the baby right now. Right now. We have to know where the baby is."

They gave temporary custody to my mother. Here's the kicker: my mother lived with me. So they gave temporary custody to my mother, which meant my daughter would live in my house, with me. I just don't get it. If you think I'm a danger, then what the hell? It's just on paper. In the court documents, it read: "Daughter was taken away from her immediately." No, she wasn't! I breastfed her until she was eight months old.

The cops showed up at the door one day—Jamie was around eight months old—and I was extradited back to my home state. The people in charge of transporting me told everyone in the van that I had killed my two children. I was on my period at the time, and they refused to provide me with a change of pad, so by the time we got to the prison, I had bled through my clothes.

"Baby killer," one of the female guards said as I got off the van.

I was assigned a public defender who insisted that I have a sleep study done at a medical center. I got a full night's sleep the night before and went to the center early in the morning. They hooked me up to these machines, and I was there all day and night. The study found that it takes my body less than two seconds to fall into REM sleep. I was diagnosed with severe narcolepsy.

I was officially charged with two counts of first-degree murder, special circumstance. That means that if I were to have been found guilty of murder, I would have been eligible for the death penalty or, at the very least, life in prison without the possibility of parole. Time and time again, the charges would get dropped and the DA would bring new charges. He and the detective on the case really had it out against me, thought that I had murdered my children.

That same detective was the one who convinced the coroner to change his findings on my son's death from SIDS to asphyxiation. The firefighters told me that it was SIDS, but the coroner's report stated that the baby was alive when the firefighters arrived. That really changes things. It puts the blame on me.

A bunch of judges wouldn't take my case. They watched after their own political aspirations and played hot potato with my life. But the DA was tenacious: a case like mine had never been tried in my state, so it set a precedent. I guess that's another reason that he pushed so hard. The judge kept throwing the cases out, and I kept getting recharged, each time with a different crime. What finally stuck was one count of child abuse and endangerment.

The judge said to the DA, "If you're charging her with abuse, show me the abuse." The DA argued that sitting on the bed with my baby, in light of what had happened to my son, was the act of child abuse. Had she been there in the room with me that day, she argued, she would have had me arrested.

The process of being charged with a crime, and the legal counsel I received throughout, was very confusing to me. I grew up in a hardworking, low-income American family. My brothers and I would glean fields for change and get penny candies, and we thought life was good. Before my first child died, I was making $25,000 a year and I was happy—I thought I was rich.

My family, you know, we've always had this deep, unshakable belief in fairness and justice. When I was diagnosed with narcolepsy, everyone was relieved, myself included. I remember my brother hugging me and saying, "I knew you were innocent," over and over again. So when I got charged with child abuse and endangerment, I guess we were all just confused. If I am innocent, then why am I being treated like a criminal? Why am I still facing prison time?

My lawyer urged me to plead "no contest" to one count of child abuse and endangerment. He kept saying—Don't you want to go back home, to your old life, to your kid?—and I kept thinking, *Yes, of course, I do. But why can't I just plead not guilty?*

He told me, "If you plead not guilty, we take the case to a jury trial, and if you're found guilty, you'll get fifteen years in prison. So just plead no contest and the judge can make the decision." A couple of times throughout the process, he told me to cry so that I came off more sympathetic. I guess he thought I wasn't emotional enough. The detective who was in charge of my case came to the hearings, too—he wanted to make sure he followed through, saw me put away.

Everyone around me seemed to be more involved in my case— seemed to care more than I did. I was numb. I had no fight left in me. So it seemed like a good idea to just take the plea deal, serve the time, and not make any more trouble for myself. I ended up serving two and a half years of a ten-year sentence in prison. Six years were suspended, but I was still on probation. I took the plea because it meant seeing Jamie on her fourth birthday, instead of her sixteenth.

The whole thing is a blur. I don't think I was given bad counsel, but I just had no idea what I was doing, what my rights were, or the implications of the charges on my future. I didn't know that pleading no contest is basically like saying, *Yeah, the DA has the facts right, I'm just not going to admit I'm guilty*. I was in a haze; I trusted my lawyer too much. It's like the first time you play a game: you obviously lose because you don't know what you're doing. But how many times does your life actually hang in the balance?

I look back on this now and all I can think is: *If they truly thought that I abused and killed my babies, then shouldn't I be getting the death penalty? Shouldn't I rot away in prison for the rest of my life? How could I be charged with doing something so heinous, so evil, and only get a slap on the wrist? That's getting away with murder. Twice.*

I grew up believing in America, believing in our justice system. Maybe that was naive; I don't know. After what I went through, I don't think our justice system is just racist. I think it's classist. If you're not educated, if you don't know your rights, if you're poor and can't afford to pay for your representation, then your life can be taken away from you in a heartbeat.

My mother permanently adopted Jamie. She never let her move back in with me. I have two other kids now. Because of my narcolepsy, I can't work. I can't drive. I'm on a bunch of medication: Adderall, Lyrica, Baclofen, and the list goes on. I don't have the mental ability to do very much because I'm broken.

Every mom imagines, when she's pregnant, *What will my baby look like? What will they accomplish?* You daydream all kinds of things. In my head, my kids had lived full and perfect lives. I'd seen them graduate from high school, go to college, and meet the loves of their lives. I had hopes for them, and I loved them.

If I talk about my children, I'll always have a broken heart. If I talk about the justice system, I get angry. I live a life that's filled with pain, not guilt.

Leila, early thirties

Ever since I was a little girl, I knew that I wanted to become a mother one day. A couple of years after my husband and I got married, we decided to start trying for a baby. We had dated for over fifteen years, so we never felt like, *Oh, we need us time.* We'd held off for a little while for logistical and financial reasons, so I knew that because I was already in my early thirties, it might be a little difficult for us to conceive. I'm very much a realist and a type A control freak, so from the very first month that we were trying, I had a thermometer and I'd check my temperature every morning to see when I was ovulating. It made my husband crazy.

"What is this, a science experiment?" he'd ask. "Why are you already acting like something is not working?"

But I found it empowering and exciting to know about my body.

We were really lucky. We conceived on the second month of trying. I'd been taking pregnancy tests early on because I knew exactly when I'd been ovulating. The night before I found out I was pregnant, my husband and I fought. I'd taken a test and the result was negative, so we argued because I wasn't being "chill"—I'd made it into a whole hullabaloo. But the morning after, I decided to take another test. I saw that faint pink line, and I was overjoyed. I was crying tears of happiness in the shower, and I was just really at peace because the news was all mine for a little while. I managed to keep the secret all day and I stopped by Target on the way home from work and bought a onesie. That night, I gave it to my husband. And that's where our story began.

Now that I look back on it, there were definitely signs that didn't seem normal, but it was my first time being pregnant, so I had nothing to compare it to. I remember going on a walk around my neighborhood and talking to my mom and telling her that I had really bad cramps. It was all on my left side. I tend to be so negative and anxious, so I made a concerted effort to not get sucked into Dr. Google. I tried to stay positive: *Maybe my uterus is stretching or it's implantation cramping, or . . .*

A few weeks later, I noticed that I was spotting, but I'd read that this was a common side effect of pregnancy, too. The next day at work, right after lunch, I went to the bathroom and I noticed some bright red blood on my underwear. I was scared, but I composed myself and texted my sister-in-law, who has two kids. I figured she would tell me that I was just being a worrywart, but she advised me to talk to my doctor. She didn't dismiss the issue like I thought she would—she actually seemed concerned—and that's when I really started worrying. I went home early from work and waited for my appointment the next day.

That appointment was . . . *oh boy* . . . something else. I was still trying to be positive; I even said to my husband, "We're going to see the baby today."

The ultrasound tech came in and she was very perfunctory— she told me to take off my underwear and cover myself with a sheet. I don't remember if the lights were on or off at that point, but she didn't give any indication that she planned on leaving the room to let me get undressed in privacy. I thought that was strange, but I wanted to get on with it, so I lay down and she started doing a vaginal ultrasound. She wasn't saying much, just moving the wand around, so I asked, "Do you see anything?"

She said, "Your uterus is empty."

And then she pulled the wand out of me and held it in plain sight as she removed the disposable sheath. It was covered in blood. There was no small talk, no comfort. She didn't even give me a wipe. So I put my underwear back on and started crying. Without giving us a moment to process anything, she ushered us out to the lobby, where we waited for our doctor. A few minutes later, the doctor came out and told us that we should give it time, to go to lunch somewhere, and "see what happens," but that it was most likely a miscarriage. She told me to come back the next day.

I know that we all do our jobs, which are but a small portion of our lives. I know that it's hard, we're all human, and you can't be your best self every minute of every day. But I'm not sure I'll ever be able to forget how I was treated that day.

Later that same night, I had a lot more cramping and bleeding and I felt in my gut, *Okay, I'm having a miscarriage.* I was on the toilet and at one point, I felt something pass. I remember feeling it physically coming out of me and it being really intense—I felt crazy. I wasn't sure if that was my baby. I don't remember if I flushed it or put it in the waste bin, but I remember that I started sobbing.

At the doctor's the next day, they told me that my uterine lining was thin and it looked like I was having a miscarriage. I had a journal with me, and in the waiting room at the doctor's office while we waited to be checked out, I wrote a letter to our baby—I had a feeling that she was a girl—and said goodbye. I wrote, *I can't wait to meet you at the end of life, and I love you very much.* Even though it was a small amount of time that she lived in me, I was trying to honor that momentary life.

We went down to the beach a few days later and brought some flowers and put them in the ocean. Watching them float away was our way of saying goodbye and having some closure.

I had already "classified" the event as a miscarriage, and I tried my best to process everything and move forward. But one afternoon, as I was driving home from work, I was in so much pain that I had to pull over. My husband picked me up because I was sobbing and physically couldn't drive. My body was telling me, *This is not normal, something else is going on.*

A few days later, I had another doctor's appointment to check that my HCG levels had gone down. My doctor did another ultrasound, and told me there was nothing to worry about. She said there was a cyst in one of my ovaries but "maybe you're about to get your period." She seemed really dismissive, but at this point we felt like we had no option but to trust her.

My husband asked, "Is there any way this could be an ectopic?" We had spent a couple of sleepless nights reading about research studies done on ectopic pregnancies and HCG levels by the NIH. We knew that it was a super rare and possibly dangerous (for the mother) case in which the egg implants outside the uterus, usually in the fallopian tube. The pregnancy would not be viable. Could we be one of the 2 percent? She said it was really unlikely. That was Friday.

On Monday, she called me with my test results. She said, "I got your number. It looks good." And when she told me what it was, I realized that my HCG levels were actually higher than they had been two weeks prior.

And I said "What, how is that *good*? It's higher. I had a miscarriage. How is that possible?"

After a couple of confused seconds during which she probably looked up what my HCG levels had been before and realized her error, she said, "Well, maybe you should come in and we can give you methotrexate injections."

At this point, my mind is blown and I am *angry*. Our doctor was younger than most of the others in the practice, and she had always seemed flippant and dismissive, but this was above and beyond irresponsible. I probably prevented her from committing medical malpractice. If I hadn't read up online and caught the rise in my HCG levels, I could have had a ruptured ectopic and bled to death. It could have left me unable to have children. Her lapse would have changed our lives forever.

And she didn't even seemed fazed. She basically said, *In that case, okay, come in, get chemo, and kill your baby.* I was so distraught—it finally *being confirmed* that it was an ectopic was not a shock because my husband and I had *known* it, somehow. But my doctor's attitude, how casual it seemed to her to tell me to come in and terminate the pregnancy . . . it was baffling.

She wanted me to make the decision to come in and terminate the pregnancy fairly quickly due to the risk of a ruptured fallopian. I'm actually very proud of how I handled the moments that followed. I was very conflicted because if it had just been a miscarriage, well, that's fairly common and you don't have to do anything—your body just spontaneously aborts the fetus. But ectopics are not common. And it almost got missed. *And* I had to go in and get the chemo shot to basically end it—dissolve it—whatever the word is. That was really difficult for me given how much I wanted this child, how much I wanted to be a mother. I have to live with that choice. The way that I rationalized it is that I knew this child would not survive. It was not a choice between me or the baby, because if it had been, I would have picked the baby. It was not me *and* not the baby.

It was hard for my husband to try again. He knew that the odds of having another ectopic were pretty low since I don't have any risk factors. It was just a fluke. Bad luck. The silver lining is that the experience solidified how lucky we are to have each other. My husband—as much as he is Mr. Positive and I am Negative Nelly—let me share whatever I was feeling whenever I was feeling it. And it was a lot, because I carried that pain for a long time. It was his pain, too, and for him to listen patiently as I brought it up whenever I needed to, it was crucial for me. That's the only way I managed not to lose my mind from grief.

I remember the day I found out we were pregnant again. I went in to the doctor's—different doctor!—super early to see if they could see a sac because I was at higher risk due to the first ectopic. Before going into the office, I prayed to the first little one and told her to watch over her little brother or sister. And then I prayed to God and I said, "Okay, this is it, God. It's going to be good. You're not going to take this one away from me. I'm not asking you. I'm telling you." And then afterward, when I knew everything was okay, I apologized. I said, "I know I'm not special, and I don't command results, but thank you for letting me have this one."

I might be telling a different story if I wasn't pregnant now. I'm really excited and happy, and it buffers the sadness we felt for so long. I don't want to forget that this happened to me. I don't want to erase it because no matter what, she will always be my first child.

Selma, twenties

I'm nervous. Every time I've told this story, no one has believed me.

My brother had a best friend, Scott, who would always come over and hang out. One day, during the summer, he and my brother were playing video games in the living room. Scott got up to use the bathroom, and I was hanging out in the kitchen, alone. My older sister wasn't around. When he was done in the bathroom, he closed the door really quietly and tiptoed into the kitchen. He reached out and touched my chest and then, really clumsily, he tried to kiss me. Then he went back to play video games. I didn't really make a big deal out of it. I was ten or eleven. I liked Scott all right, and the girls in my class had already started talking about kissing boys.

A few months went by with nothing to report, and then that fall, we had a guest speaker at school who came to talk to us about abstinence. Scott came over to our house after school, and I remember he made some comment about how he thought it was a good idea to be abstinent. While we were all hanging out, Scott kept messing with me, always reaching over and poking me or giving me a hug. My mom had a bunch of friends over; they were all downstairs playing cards while my brother, Scott, and I watched TV upstairs. Eventually, we all went to bed. Scott slept over in my brother's room.

I don't know how he got my shorts and underwear down without me waking up, but the first thing I remember is him pushing, and then the pain. I could see part of his face. He had his hand over my mouth, and because he was using both arms to hold his weight up, the hand that was covering my mouth was actually pushing my head down into my mattress painfully. I hit him over and over and then he stopped for a second. I thought maybe he was finished, but

I noticed he was searching for something in his pocket. Scott and my brother were outdoorsy boys, and I realized that he'd pulled out the pocketknife that he always carried around. I didn't see it so much as I heard him open it, and then he put it on my neck.

What I remember very clearly was that when he started there was some light in the room because I could see part of his face. But when he finished, the light was blocked. I looked over at the doorframe and I could make out my brother's silhouette.

I remember hearing my mom and her friends laughing downstairs. I was scared that Scott would hurt me again, so I didn't move even after he left. When my parents came upstairs for the night, I made myself stop crying because I didn't want them to ask me any questions. The next day, there was blood on my sheets, so I told my mom that I thought I'd gotten my period. She taught me how to use a pad and then, a few months later, I actually got my period.

Six months after I was raped, I walked into my room to find my mother sobbing as she read my diary. I had written about what had happened but left out names. She asked me if it was true, and I told her it was. She asked me who it was, and I said it was Scott. She said she had figured. She called the police. They asked me questions and took my diary. My mom was in pieces. She asked me what she should do. She was too distraught to console me, so I got up, went to her, and I hugged her. And I told her I was okay.

The next day, I went to get a pelvic exam. The doctors told my mom that there was scarring. I remember my mom looked at me like there was something wrong with me. A few months later, she told me that the DA had dropped the case. So nothing ever came of it.

After everything came to light, I told my brother that I had seen him by the doorway, watching. He got angry and started screaming that Scott was innocent, but I could tell by the look in his face that I was right. I hadn't imagined it. He had been watching.

My mother and I didn't talk about what happened again until I was eighteen. We were fighting—we often do—and she asked me whether I had "given it to him" and then had gotten scared because I'd lost my virginity. When I got angry and upset, she straight out said she didn't believe me—she accused me of lying about it. My sister has also never believed that anything happened. We used to watch a lot of Lifetime movies together and many of them dealt with rape. They're pretty formulaic: the victims are questioned, and nobody believes them in the beginning. But in the movies, the rapist always ends up getting in trouble if it really happened.

"So why would you wait six months?" my sister wanted to know.

I told her I'd never planned on saying a thing, that Mom had found out. I said I'd been too scared. She said that if it was her, she would have told.

I saw Scott at a local restaurant once, years later, and I went into the bathroom and started hyperventilating. He works with children now. I worry about the kids all the time. I called his employer and tried to warn them about him. They said they hadn't had a problem, and if there were no charges brought, there was nothing that they could do. I often blame myself for not saying anything—if I had told on him that night and the police had evidence, he wouldn't be allowed around children today.

My brother still lives with my mother. He isn't doing well. Whenever I think about him, my gut tells me that it's only a matter of time before he kills himself. I don't blame him very much because he was molested by our half brother when he was younger. Our half brother was caught in the act by our parents, but it was swept under the rug. They sent my brother to counseling for two years, but anyone could tell he was never himself again—he used to try to force himself into the bathroom with me. My mom caught him one time, and she must have scared him bad, because he stopped. He probably deals with a lot of guilt from doing those things and letting Scott rape me. I remember I read a statistic once that half the Americans who have been molested will do it to someone else. Well, that makes me feel so sick. I am overwhelmed by sadness for my brother, who was a young boy himself when he was victimized. And I am sad for myself, too.

I know that for at least part of what happened, my brother feels guilty. He's told me that he's sorry once before. He kind of looked at me one day and out of the blue said, "I'm really sorry." I asked him what for. He just turned and walked away. I've told him that I forgive him, and I think I do. I know that I don't blame him, so I don't know if there's much to forgive, because it wasn't his fault.

As for me, well, I have PTSD. During the day, snippets of that night flash into my head—the sliver of hallway light that cut a diagonal line into my room, the knife on my neck and the sound it made when he flipped it open, his hand over my mouth, and distinctly feeling like the weight of it would suffocate me. I often think about the rape exam six months later and that look on my mom's face. Most times, these flashbacks happen in the shower. I wonder why. I guess I already feel so vulnerable in the shower and that sends me over the edge? I have regular nightmares, almost every night, about what happened. I don't necessarily dream about Scott or what he did; when I wake up from the nightmare, though, the only thing on my mind is that night. I am a hypervigilant sleeper. My fiancé tells me that I swing my arms a lot, like I'm trying to punch someone. I guess it must be while I'm having a nightmare. I haven't told him about anything that happened. I'm not sure it would change things between us if I did, but I'm not sure I want him to see that part of me.

Throughout my teens, I decided that sex wasn't mine to give away anymore because it had been taken from me, and so sex, indiscriminate and careless sex, became a coping mechanism—a way to work out the pain. The other was cutting. I used to cut up and down my left arm and some on my legs, particularly on the inside of my thighs. My high school counselor noticed the scars on my arm— they darken when I'm out in the sun—and told me that I needed to tell my mom, or she would.

My mom's reaction? That I was doing it for attention. The

counselor disagreed. She said that I needed professional help be-cause I was "very obviously struggling with something." My mother was very angry, of course. When we were alone at home later that day, she told me that the next time I wanted to cut, I should do it in front of her so that she could tell me how deep to go.

I'm not sure what else to say, except that I hope you believe me. And I wish it hadn't happened.

IDENTITY

Justin, midthirties

I lost my job a couple of years ago due to a back injury, and now I'm a stay-at-home dad. I love being at home with my kids, but it's slowly killing me. I've never been without a job, and now, because of my injury, I can't provide for my family like I used to. It's a pride thing: I can no longer hunt, I can't take on odd jobs, I can't play with my boys because I can't pick them up or run after them—I feel like I'm not only less of a parent but less of a man.

My wife and I have been married for eight years, and for the first seven, we never fought. These days, her anxiety levels are through the roof. She works full-time, and she's very high-strung. I can understand that: it's a lot of psychological pressure to have to be the sole breadwinner. She's not the type of person who is super adaptable to any situation. It takes her a long time to get comfortable with new situations at work, and so she's constantly coming home with gripes about this and that. I try to talk her through things, talk her off the ledge, but she resents any advice I give her because she tells me she just "wants to vent." The thing is, the next day she's complaining about the same thing. It's like *Groundhog Day* with her—nothing ever changes, all she wants to do is complain. She's mostly unhappy at work, and I feel like she would like the option to walk away. Unfortunately, because we depend on her salary, she can't, and that's probably her chief source of resentment toward me.

After I was hurt, I filed for disability, but I was denied. It takes about fourteen to sixteen months to get a disability hearing, and when I told her that, she got so angry with me. It's not like it's something that I can control! It takes as long as it takes, but I guess she was already getting tired of me hanging around the house—she was probably hoping for an easy fix, and for things to go back to normal. When we were both working, we had a safety net. Yeah, we were paying for the kids' day care, so financially we weren't really better off, but at least the both of us got to leave the house and be adults every day. So God knows I was hoping for things to go back to normal, too. We're both under so much pressure: 90 percent of the time, she thinks I don't care about the state of our lives because I don't react to bad news the way she does. But it's not like anything would get any better if we were both freaking out.

People who knew us as a couple used to hate that we never argued. I knew my wife was "the one" when we started dating because things were easy. We didn't butt heads, there were no miscommunications, we didn't have to think twice about bringing something up—it just worked between us. Everything happened easily, organically. It was unlike any relationship I'd ever been in before. I was used to conflict, fighting every few months, minor and major disagreements. But we moved in together, got married, had kids, and we didn't really hit any bumps in the road until recently. In the past year or so, we've been fighting like crazy. Every little thing sets her off.

If I'm on my phone, she's pissed. If the dishes aren't done, the dinner cooked, the kids in bed, she's pissed. If she doesn't see me "doing something" at all times, she's pissed. And ever since we had our second son a couple of years ago, there has been no action in the bedroom at all. She doesn't show any interest in me if I don't beg and plead. It's always been me initiating. There's something about sex, about the release of it, that just sets things back to equilibrium for my soul. It's animalistic; it's evolutionarily what people need. It's what I need desperately, and to have it withheld is so emasculating. I feel like because it's sex, the lack of it isn't taken seriously. But if it were a hug that I needed, or a home-cooked meal, or a comforting cup of tea brought to me in bed—or whatever it is that makes any particular person feel seen, valued, and loved—withholding it would be seen as callous, a sign of a careless partner.

The thing is, there's a lot more expected of me now that I'm home all the time. When I was working and the kids were in day care, I never really stopped to consider what it takes to be a stay-at-home parent; it's demanding. I was working nights for the first five years of our first son's life, and so I missed out on the day-to-day work of raising him. The responsibility that I feel when I'm with my sons far outweighs anything I ever felt at my job. I have to cover the basics, which I guess is easy enough: make sure they're clean, fed, and safe. But that's the bare minimum. On top of making their food, doing the laundry, and keeping the house running (repairs, etc.), I have to also make sure our kids are thriving. That means setting up activities for them when they're at home, helping them with their homework, driving them to and from extracurriculars, and setting up playdates with other kids. Once all that is done, I'm completely exhausted. I have nothing left in me.

It takes such a toll on me to spend all day taking care of the kids. I do everything for them. And I hate to sound whiny, but raising kids these days isn't as easy as it used to be—you can't just send them to school with a Lunchable and tell them to count their lucky stars. These days, everything has to be organic and free-range and hormone-free and all that. It's easy to get sucked into this vortex of high-performance parenting because you don't want your kid to be the one who's behind. When my wife comes home, it's more of the same demands; she's tired from work, so I have to pick up the slack. I feel like I can't complain or tell her to help out, because she'll get angry and tell me to get a job, and I really can't hear that right now; my ego can't take it. I feel so beat down. I'm downhearted.

My friendships have also suffered ever since I lost my job. I'm fairly traditional as far as hobbies go—I used to enjoy hunting and fishing, watching and playing sports—and now that I can no longer do that with my friends, it's hard to find common ground. All my friends work, of course. It feels emasculating to be in a room full of dudes and to have nothing to share except what the kids did at school that day, what the kids said over breakfast, all the chores that are piling up.

I guess I'm upset because my wife isn't really articulating her appreciation for everything I do for her, the kids, and the house. I don't want a party, but it would be nice to be told once in a while that what I'm doing is noticed. That it matters. I am also an empath, an emotional sponge, so when my wife comes home in a foul mood, it really affects me. I absorb her feelings, and I take them personally and try to "solve" her problems. I am almost always overwhelmed because I feel like the emotional backbone of the family, but there's nobody there when I need support. When I think back on when the tables were turned—when she held the primary responsibility for taking care of the kids—I'm not sure that I was all that appreciative of her, though. I guess it's one of those things that has to be lived in order to be understood.

I know that what I do at home is important—not just theoretically, but financially, too. If I weren't home, we'd have to pay for day care, which would effectively cancel out one of our salaries anyways. Even so, I can't help but feel that my wife isn't sexually attracted to me anymore because I'm not "the man"—I'm not out there, providing for our family. I know that it's a double standard: men are expected to contribute around the house, fifty-fifty. Gone are the days when women worked and took care of the house and kids. And gone are the days when women were expected to stay at home. But now that the tables are turned and I'm contributing more than my fair share, I feel like she certainly doesn't respect me as much as she used to. My stock has definitely gone down in her book. I'm at home watching the kids and playing house—basically, I'm a housewife. It's hard to find a housewife sexy.

My mom, God rest her soul, she was a white-knuckles type of person. I want to pick up the phone and call her, ask for her advice. It's been two years since she died, and I still have images of her last day—the way that her skin looked, the way she took my hand just before she was going to pass, like she was afraid of being alone. I miss her. She was my best friend. I need her wisdom now more than ever because I feel like my life is slipping away from me. Whether I liked it or not, my job defined me. It took up my time and made me feel like I was a productive member of society because I got a check every two weeks and paid my taxes. Without a job, I don't know who I am anymore. I love my kids, but being their caretaker just isn't enough.

I don't know how long my wife and I can go on like this before something happens—before we disintegrate. And there is so much at stake—our family, the kids. I can't let that happen.

Maddy, early thirties

One look at me, and people think I'm privileged. And in a lot of ways I am, because I'm white, I sound educated, and I can get unskilled jobs pretty easily. I let people see what they want—I conform to the picture of me that's easiest to digest. It's neater than the truth. People just don't feel the need to dig because I don't send up red flags—at worst, they assume I am harmless and bland; at best, my image tells them I am competent, educated, worthy, superior. It's amazing how big a part appearances play in success.

I grew up poor in America—in a dilapidated house in the middle-of-nowhere Texas Hill Country, with no running water, no heat, very little food, and no medical or dental care for miles and miles around. I went to school with the wealthy kids from the suburbs of Austin. They all assumed I was just like them. High school taught me to fit in, to be a social chameleon—to take on the look and mannerisms of my peers. But they wore nice clothes, drove the nicest cars, and lived in mansions, while I often went to bed hungry and wore the soles off an old pair of shoes. People only see what they want to, though. They thought I was just like them, and anything that didn't fit into that narrative was dismissed as an eccentricity, a quirk. In a school as big as mine, it was easy to hide in plain sight. I got used to being glossed over, being painted in the broadest of strokes. It worked in my favor—not being seen.

It's hard to believe that poverty—real poverty like the one I lived through—still exists in America. That's why I don't tell anyone about my childhood, and it's also probably why I'm always eating or snacking as an adult. It's a survival mechanism that's left over from that fear I had as a kid that we wouldn't have enough food that night. It's also why I'm such a private person. My mom was deeply ashamed of the way we lived. She worked her whole life, but it still wasn't enough to break even. I still carry my mother's shame. It became my shame.

She was so secretive about our home and financial situation that she never let me have any friends over. The one time that a school friend did happen to visit, it was really obvious that she didn't know what to make of me now that she had this context. It seemed like she didn't know how to act, and I became really self-conscious. Was she judging me? Did she feel sorry for me? She just seemed so uncomfortable, almost like she didn't want to sit down because she thought we were dirty. We were poor, not dirty! I immediately regretted having invited her, and I never had anyone over again.

When I was in my early twenties, I got out. My best friend moved to a big city, and I followed her. I started working—hustling and scraping by, often holding down several jobs at once—and I felt normal for the first time because I was in a city where so many people did the same thing. It wasn't weird that I was a white girl in the back of the restaurant, washing dishes and mopping floors in a room where English was the foreign language. Work is work. I never felt too good or above it. It wasn't weird that I was sharing a one-bedroom with two other people because everyone my age was in the same position. I told myself that it was the grind, that we were all in the same boat. I felt assimilated. But I still have lingering hang-ups from my past, and I often feel like an impostor in my new life—like if I try for more than I'm worth, people will see right through me. Maybe washing dishes in the back room is where I belong. Maybe unskilled labor is where I top off. Or maybe I allow myself to think that because it makes it okay if I fail out here. They'll see the girl I used to be. The girl I am, I guess.

I never moved away from home with the intention of "making it" elsewhere—but it's how I tell the story (to myself) now. I don't like to think about home because it depresses me, where I came from. It's the sort of memory that I lock away and only visit when I'm about to fall asleep and the anxiety gets to me. Home is kind of like my "or else." I better get this job, "or else." I better make rent, "or else." It's an alternative that scares me enough to want to do better.

But people also assume I have a safety net to fall back on if I fail. And that's as far as that illusion of being "in the same boat" will carry me. Whenever I'm struggling, my friends ask why I don't just hit my parents up for help. They can do it, sure: one call to Mom and Dad and rent is paid. One call, and they can afford to spend $8 on a small ice cream, or $5 on a latte, or $12 on a green juice. So, yeah, they're sharing that one bedroom with me, but the difference between me and them is that I don't have a choice. They do it as an experiment in independence, in hacking it on their own in the big city.

In the way that some of my friends speak about their lives, I can tell that they take certain things for granted—nice childhood homes, a family who loves them, and a place to turn to when things go south. It confuses me because I look just like them, but I feel so different. You wouldn't believe how many times I've heard the word *unconditional* associated with parents. For me, it's so far from the truth. My friends think that my refusal to ask for help is noble, is principled. They don't get that not all parents are the same.

I talk to my mom every once in a while, whenever I'm feeling brave enough to confront some real issues. Like, for example, why she harbored an emotionally abusive man in our house for so long. My stepfather crushed whatever was left of my self-esteem, and for the longest time I couldn't talk about my feelings. He mocked me, so I clowned around—made jokes, deflected questions, acted tough. Even so many years later, I'm still not ready to let anyone in, to let them see the mess.

I read somewhere that the number one predictor of a woman's earning capacity is her father's income and occupation. If I take that at face value, then no matter what I do, my childhood has conditioned me for a life lived in poverty. I know many people think that getting an education and finding a good, steady job can change that—but these opportunities are not within arm's reach for all Americans. The idea of putting myself into student loan debt and forgoing several years' worth of a salary only to hopefully get a better job in this market is not all too appealing.

But I don't say this to most people. There's so much criticism directed at millennials nowadays that any whisper of a complaint draws out mass accusations of entitlement—even where it doesn't exist. The preferred narrative is all about the bootstraps stories, the easy tales of people who struggled but then they just pulled themselves together and made it. Just like that.

And that's a pretty story to tell, sure. But it's also dangerous and misleading. For every one of them, there are hundreds of me— people who have seen just how far you can fall, who have experienced what it's like to go to sleep hungry, and who have nowhere to turn to for help but inward. I've been on the verge of homelessness, on the verge of hunger, and on the verge of unemployment. On any given day, my life has as much of a chance of being a bootstrap narrative as it does of being a cautionary tale.

These days, most of my peers come from affluent or middle-class homes. Through no fault of their own, they project their reality onto mine. They assume that I grew up similarly, had similar luxuries and toys, and lived a childhood that mirrors theirs. A while back, I was in the kitchen with my roommate and she was using this fancy apple-slicing contraption. I asked her about it, and she said something to the effect of "they sold these in infomercials back in the day; everyone had one of these," and all I could think was that we barely even had apples. She called me a simpleton.

I often tell myself that my upbringing built character and that I'm better for it. I'm more empathetic, well-rounded, understanding, approachable, strong. Some days, that doesn't ring true. Some days, I want my life to have been simple. I want everything to have come easily, and why not? What's so wrong with an easy life? I don't want to begrudge my friends their luck, but sometimes I do. Sometimes I want to get in the shower and scrub away my past from my skin, get myself unstuck from my thoughts, let all the bad slide off. Sometimes I feel like if I scrub hard enough, if I change things around just so, I'll get to the girl who everyone sees.

You know, in most chick flicks I've ever watched, there's that character of the girl who has it all—perfect husband, perfect job, perfect style, perfect hair. At some point in the course of the movie, that character ends up breaking down and showing that things aren't so perfect in her life, after all. Well, I think that's a BS plot device. Some people do have it all. I see them every day in their designer shoes, having lunch with their pretty friends, posting up photos of their summer adventures. And I struggle with my prejudice against them. But maybe they're just showing me what I want to see, too.

I wish there was a label you could wear that told people everything they needed to know about you. I feel like it would make people so much kinder to one another—to know of people's troubles and burdens, and be more considerate of them. Mine would say— Maddy: good person, hard worker, grew up poor. Trying her best.

Marc, fifty-one

This is hard to talk about because I grew up in a very conservative Christian environment. Currently, I work for a Christian organization where my morality and status as an upstanding citizen is probably the most important factor in my continued employment.

My first encounter with my sexuality was when I was eleven or twelve. I found a stash of *Playboy* magazines out in the woods behind my house. I brought one copy back and hid it under my bed. I was fascinated by it, but initially it was asexual. Once I figured out what I could do, though, I began to develop an unhealthy obsession with the female form. There was one woman in particular, her name was Candy Loving, who was very well endowed. She had a 34D bra size, and that size, specifically, is a trigger for me—that's what I'm attracted to. I would masturbate to the magazine one or two times a day.

In college, things were pretty normal. I met Ali during my senior year of school, and she also had a 34D chest. She was very conservative and uncomfortable with her sexuality, but I started to encourage her to show off her body more. I would pick out her outfits for her, and she was getting a lot of attention from guys. Men would look at her—it was obvious that she was having an effect. She would tell me how it made her feel, and we kind of continued the "conversation" back home. It turned her on, getting attention from other men. We got married and went on our honeymoon to Hawaii. Before the honeymoon, we went bikini shopping together.

We'd been married for a couple of years when she told me that this guy at work was hitting on her. With my permission, she went out with him and eventually they had sex. She came home and told me about it and compared him to me. It was exciting, being compared and feeling, sometimes, humiliated or not good enough—it turned me on. She was out on another date with him, and I was at home, thinking about what they might be saying and doing, and I got really turned on. I started playing around with her underwear and her bra. And then I tried them on. She came home and found me with her things on, and she was very critical. She thought it was not all right. Well, that was the beginning of the end with Ali. After things ended with us, she started dating—in the traditional sense— the guy at work. They're married now, and they have a big, beautiful family.

When I was going through the divorce with Ali, I went out and bought a bunch of magazines and was masturbating in my car during the day. A woman walked by and saw me, and I got arrested for indecent exposure even though I was minding my business in my car, and I didn't expose myself knowingly. I got a probation before judgment—so two years of probation, and if it didn't happen again, it would be expunged from my record. I wanted to get away from the East Coast, away from the divorce and the mess I'd made for myself legally, so I decided to move out to California.

During this same time, email and the internet became more available. I started using the internet for porn, and it began to feed my addiction and my fantasies. I also started to pay for phone sex. I went to hotels that were frequented by prostitutes in order to act out my fantasies. Every last dime I made was going toward fulfilling my sexual desires. During a binge, I'd go to multiple prostitutes and strip clubs two or three times a day. In one day, I could easily spend my entire paycheck and anything I might have managed to save during a few days that I'd tried to restrain myself. Thousands of dollars—poof.

In California, I had a stroke of bad luck. Someone I knew through Ali came to one of my work events. She knew about my kinks, brought them to my boss, and I got fired. I decided to move back east and started working for my alma mater.

These were two of the best years of my life. I'd started getting some counseling and going to Sex Addicts Anonymous. Plus, there wasn't much happening in my small town in terms of strip clubs and other temptations. But the internet was still a problem, so I began to compartmentalize in order to gain some more self-control. I'd only release on certain days, and I had a maximum spending limit. It didn't always work, but things seemed better. I met a girl, we got engaged, and I had the opportunity to move to a big city for a dream job. Obviously, along with the big-city paycheck came the big-city temptations.

There was an adult bookstore on the side of the road just outside the city. I was out there for business, and I was driving back home when I saw it for the first time. I made a U-turn and sat in the parking lot for about ten, fifteen minutes. But I went in. All the feelings and temptations cropped back up out of their neat little compartments. In the back of the store, there was an "arcade" area—very dark, private, and with curtains. There were lots of men back there, strolling around. I went into one of the booths and started masturbating. The booths had holes in the walls, glory holes—these are mostly for gay men, and they're very illegal. These places get raided all the time. I was too scared to do anything, so I just finished and ran out.

I started to engage in increasingly risky behavior after that. In my experience, sexual fantasies are progressive. You get a high, the dopamine levels spike, but then there's only so many times you can look at and experience the same thing before you want to take it up a notch. It happens little by little. For example, I never had the obsession with bras and panties growing up. That really came out, full blast, when I was in the cuckold marriage.

Looking for the next thing, I started calling phone-sex services again and one night I got hold of this woman. I told her about my obsession with women's lingerie, and she started telling me that I'm not much of a man. She was emasculating me, and it really got me off. I called her several times in the span of a few weeks, and she progressively got in my head about telling my fiancée about what I was up to. She wasn't doing it out of concern, of course—it was just another sexual ploy. She asked for my phone number. The first few times, I didn't give it to her. I gave her a fake number. It was like Samson and Delilah—why would I give in to this woman's seduction and give her so much power over me?

But eventually, in a moment of weakness, I gave in and gave her my real number. She called my fiancée and told her, and I was in the house at the time with my fiancée, watching her reaction. I know that it was a whacked-out, really terrible thing to do, but I was turned on. So I guess that's where my self-destruction fetish flourished, and I think that, later on, it grew into enjoying being financially blackmailed. Needless to say, my fiancée broke off the engagement.

I kept a low profile for a couple of months and eventually started dating again. I met this girl, got married, and we moved in together. I kept everything a secret from her, but I started wearing a bra and panties underneath my work clothes, and I started going back to that roadside bookstore. One night, after work, I went into one of the booths and some guy stuck his penis through the hole. I reached out and touched it, and I kept telling myself—*You're a girl, you can do this*—so I put him in my mouth and sucked him off for a while, until I came. The guilt I felt when I came really overwhelmed me, so I went around the side of the building and threw up. But the draw of the booth was always there, in the back of my mind. I went back a few weeks later. This guy knocks on the door, and I let him in. He tells me that I look pretty, and to "be a good girl." Those phrases are triggers for me. I gave him a blow job, and he finished on my face and immediately left. I sat there and masturbated, and the second I came I was overwhelmed by shame and self-hate.

This whole time, I'm working for this Christian organization and I have a job where everyone thinks I'm devout, on the straight and narrow. Meanwhile, I'm spending all my money and time just figuring out what perverse thing I'll get up to next.

I was being so reckless, and I felt guilty because of my wife, too. I had stopped having sex with her when I became sexually active with men. She kept asking me what was the matter—and one night, I told her some selective parts, mostly just about the cross-dressing kink. So. That's two divorces, if you're counting, and one broken-off engagement.

Since the small-town life had been good to me before, I fled my problems again and found a quaint little place in the South. They still have internet and phones in the South, though. I'd call in and tell the women who I really was, where I really worked, and that whole thing—the power dynamic, the threat of being outed—became my next fantasy. I got back in touch with my ex-fiancée. The relationship became sexual again, and she started recording all our conversations and keeping screenshots. She asked me to send her photos of myself with bra and panties on, and she started to blackmail me by threatening to put them on xHamster, this online porn website. I eventually told her that I wanted it to end and that I could no longer afford to pay her.

Weeks later, I got called in to work and they had a folder filled with photos of me—the ones I'd sent to my ex. Apparently, she had tipped them off. I tried to explain that I was being blackmailed, but nobody seemed very interested in my sob story, and who can blame them? I drove down to the road to a random strip mall parking lot and started masturbating. I had this explosive orgasm, thinking about what had happened—about actually being exposed.

I contacted a lawyer who sealed the record, and I went away quietly. I got another job, moved yet again, and checked myself into an inpatient sexual-addiction clinic. They taught me some strategies that have helped—for instance, I went back to the practice of compartmentalizing, and I try to stick to a budget. It's not about being perfect but about coping with my issue the best I can.

I reconnected with my high school sweetheart in the meantime, and we got married. So here I am. Fifty-one. Married three times. No children of my own, and maybe that's for the best.

I just don't want to be anything like my own dad. I remember when I was five years old, I was naked in the shower with my father and he was explaining his body parts to me. I don't remember if he had an erection, but I do remember that he wanted to have a "shower lesson" again, and I felt very uncomfortable about that. When I was about nine or ten, he started to come into my room before sleep to tickle my back. One time, he went below my waistband, and I felt his hand on the crack of my rear end. I turned around and I said, "What are you doing? What are you—gay?" He was stunned and taken aback, and he said no and left. And then, when I was fifteen years old, he came out as gay and divorced my mother. He's been with the same guy for thirty-plus years. So it seems that the sins of my father have been uniquely passed on to me: he was arrested in the seventies for public masturbation, too. Ultimately, I don't walk around in my "normal" life attracted to men, but sometimes I think that's what's kept me from openly exploring my sexuality—the hatred that I have for my dad.

This past month, I paid $300 for a transformation. This woman came to my hotel room, shaved my legs, did my makeup, and put a wig on me. She took photos of me in my lingerie, and she told me to leave the hotel as my alter ego, Julia. It was so thrilling, liberating. My wife was out of town, so I walked up to my condo as Julia, as well. I walked around our home and imagined what it would be like to live in this skin forever. But I know, eventually, I have to go back to real life—and real life is a constant state of suspense.

Any time that I'm at work and I get a call from my boss, I get gripped by fear. *This is it*, I think. *They've found out again*. But just as soon as that fear settles in, it's supplanted by arousal and excitement. Maybe getting found out is a chance to start over again, to start fresh. And that's not so bad.

Linda, fifties

I met him at work. I was twenty-three and he was thirty-two. We grew up in the same state, and we had the same interests. Things were good, so we got married. I picked someone who I thought could take care of me. I assumed that every husband would be like my father—honest, judicious, a good family man.

We had a good life—my husband was always so label- and image-conscious, very generous and extravagant with gifts. I remember when we first started dating, we played this game—let's tell each other a flaw about ourselves.

I said, "I have a tendency to gain weight."

And without missing a beat, he said, "How much?"

I guess I also had some peach fuzz back in the day, and he took to calling me Groucho Marx. He was that kind of guy.

My husband owned his own business, and he provided well. I was a housewife throughout our seventeen-year marriage. I was very focused on our girls and being a good mom to them. We lived in a 1.3-million-dollar home. I'd start the day with nine holes or some tennis and then sit by the pool. I was happy to be able to stay home with my girls, but I always kept my connection to work and the outside world. I always had something on the side, I guess because I felt that things might fall apart. I'm Henny Penny secretly, but I'm a practicing optimist.

One day, out of the blue—to me, at least—the IRS came knocking. We were behind on our corporate taxes. Then 9/11 happened and he lost Cantor Fitzgerald, his biggest client. We cut down on some luxuries but, for all I knew, it was business as usual. In 2005, I noticed that he was drinking more, and I didn't know why. It turned out that over the past few years, he'd used the girls' college funds and all our savings to keep the business afloat. Oh, and the house was being foreclosed on. And I was just the stupid housewife asking, "Are we okay? Can I do anything?" while our lives burned to the ground.

I can't tell you how it happened—how I spent seventeen years with someone and had absolutely no idea what he was doing. How was I so comfortable just handing over our whole livelihood to this man, trusting that he wouldn't get us into trouble, or at least trusting that he would tell me when he got us into trouble? I was so ashamed in our little town—everyone knew what happened to us and kept their distance, like our misfortune was contagious.

In marrying my husband, I was probably mimicking the dynamic in my family growing up. My mom was sick a lot, and my dad didn't want her to exert herself too much, so she didn't work for much of our childhood. When she did find a job, it was part-time, as a receptionist at her doctor's office—and it was after us kids had moved out. I guess my dad felt that if she did get sick and need medical attention, this was the best place for her to be. She moved on from her little job at the office, though, and eventually started working full-time—she was able to bridge her pension and retired well. But it took a lot of time for the family to get used to seeing her as a career woman, as someone more than a sick mom.

My husband was kind of the same. He never wanted me to have a paying job because he told me it reflected poorly on his business—that his wife "had" to work. And I trusted him, I did. Until he ran us into the ground. We lost everything; he got a new job and moved to the coast. Just like that, boom. Left me holding the bag, so to speak. And all my fake, rich friends dropped me, too. My parents paid for my divorce, and I spent some time feeling sorry for myself. My self-esteem really took a hit. I've always had thyroid issues, and I also had breast cancer, so my weight was up and down. I felt worthless. When you're single and in your forties, worthless is not a good way to feel.

I'd always been a child. My husband had taken care of everything. After the divorce, I got pulled over because my registration had expired. I started crying, and I told the poor cop, "My husband always took care of these things, and he's left me." My situation called for an adult in the room, though, so I learned how to pay the bills, continued raising the girls, and started working full-time. Eventually, I decided to go back to school so that I could build a career for myself.

But still, I was so used to having a man step up for me. I went to a matchmaking event, and the first person I met there was Don. We went out to coffee, and he talked my ear off. I remember thinking, *Boy, this guy just won't shut up about himself*. I definitely had no plans of seeing him again. But a couple of days after the date, I got some white roses in the mail with a long typed note stuck in between them, all about how wonderful it had been to meet me. I was so touched. On our second date, I went to Little Italy with him and we had a very nice day. We started dating, and even though my family couldn't stand him, we made it to two years. And then, out of the blue, he broke up with me. I was devastated. My mom had died, my dog had died, and my oldest daughter had gone off to college. I felt like my family was thinning out, so I was alone. Three months went by with no contact. And then he texted me, "I made the biggest mistake of my life." Long story short, we got back together, and that Christmas, he proposed with the most beautiful engagement ring. We were engaged for two and a half years when I got an email from him, breaking things off *again*. I told him the ring would be on the kitchen counter and . . . finally, I got a clean break.

I talk out of both sides of my mouth—I don't really want to be in a relationship, but I also don't like being alone. My current boyfriend was actually my neighbor for a while. Every time I'd go out to get my mail, he'd be there, trying to make small talk. Then I realized that his condo overlooked the mail room, and I teased him about us always seeming to get the mail at the same time. He finally fessed up and asked me on a date. I like him all right, and in some key ways, he is different from my ex-husband and ex-fiancé—for one, I make more than he does. But he has a lot of trouble expressing affection. We've been together for a few years, and he's never said "I love you." He buys me cards that say "I love you," but he's never actually written or spoken the words himself. And that's a big issue because I need affection to be communicated.

You know, I know that it's not going anywhere, but I can't break up with him. I can't break up with anyone. I always wait for them to leave me because I can't hurt their feelings. There was a ton of tension in the house when I was growing up. I internalized that as *I'm not lovable*—so I pick bad men, and I bend over backward to please them because I think I'd be lucky to get anyone. I know this is my pattern.

About a year ago, my boss got promoted out of her position and she gave a friend her job. I was miserable under the new management—I felt unappreciated. Plus, I went to get my master's degree when I was in my fifties and I knew that the clock was ticking for me, in terms of making moves in my career. There, I was plugged in as a middle manager, a solid performer. I could ride out my days, but I was unhappy.

I put out some feelers and started going on job interviews. I was kind of like Goldilocks—this bed is too hard; this one is too soft. I was looking for excuses not to move because I knew that a career move might end things with the neighbor. I guess I was okay with that, though—I had always worried that I was just a convenience because I lived in the same building. Plus, the neighbor is hot: he's younger than me, he has a full head of hair, and he doesn't have the middle-age spread; I mean, at my age, that's the trifecta! So what was he doing with me? Was I crazy to put work first and run the risk of losing him?

I did eventually find a job that was just right, and I took it. It meant a whole lot more money but also moving to a different city. I've been here eight months, and I absolutely love it. My boss is in her sixties; she is loving and kind. The company is smaller, and they care about their employees. I commuted for a couple of months, but I managed to sell my old condo in ten days for a profit. I moved into a beautiful rental in my new city, so—I guess—go me!

I thought, for sure, that it would end things with the neighbor, but instead he doubled down. My youngest daughter got married, and I thought he wouldn't go to the wedding as my date, but he went with a smile on his face and charmed my whole family. My ex-husband was there, of course, with his green-card wife who is a couple of decades younger than him and spends the majority of the year out of the country. Is that unkind of me to say? Whatever, after what he's done, I'm entitled to one snipe. I thought he looked so old. I guess the sins of the past caught up with him.

He did say, during his toast, "And thank you to their mother, Linda, for everything she did to raise our daughters so well." So, that was nice.

But I always tell my girls, "With your last name, don't ever not pay your taxes."

As for the neighbor, there he was, the feelings-are-for-suckers guy, dancing at my daughter's wedding and making jokes. Every time I think our relationship has run out of gas, he surprises me. I guess I would miss him if I lost him, but I endured a seventeen-year marriage going down the drain, and a five-year engagement, too. I am convinced that it will end, and I think it might be a self-fulfilling prophecy. I've learned that people leave—just wait long enough and they'll go.

So, wherever you go, there you are. I'm proud of my work. And proud of raising my girls. I'm proud that I turned things around for us and figured it out. But I wish I was in a good relationship. I need to work on myself: I'm overweight. If I lost the weight, maybe that would give me the confidence I need.

Scott, thirties

I run a successful Instagram fitness account with hundreds of thousands of followers. I spend my whole day at the gym, meal prepping, eating, training my clients, and managing my online persona. On Instagram, I post five to eight times a day during specific high-traffic hours (I use an app to schedule the posts), and I have a photographer whom I occasionally pay to take professional photos of me. I get paid to feature products, to train clients, and to create meal and workout plans for people. I don't use Photoshop, but that's only because finding a good Photoshop artist is difficult and expensive. I do have Facetune, though, and I use that to fix things here and there. And I do all this on top of my nine-to-five in law enforcement. Nobody in my life knows how tolling this is and how unhealthy it has become.

On Instagram stories, I post videos throughout the day of myself working out or making food. I also post on YouTube about twice a week—mostly recipes, workout plans, or challenges. The last challenge I did was to consume twenty thousand calories in twenty-four hours—that's when you epically overeat during a cheat day (and probably do some serious damage to your body) for the sake of views, likes, and subscribers. The point of the exercise is to show that even a huge splurge wouldn't significantly derail someone who is in fantastic shape. None of my "fans" are sitting there, worrying about what's happening to my cholesterol and blood sugar. Everything I do is meant to portray an image of strength, health, and discipline. All of it is calculated and posed.

I started working out when I was in middle school because I was getting bullied. I was a very small kid, I wasn't too athletic, and I had a slight stutter that showed up when I was anxious or upset. I got picked on a ton, and that made school really unpleasant for me, so I started acting out at home. I was the youngest of my brothers, so I always felt like the runt of the litter, as though I didn't matter. Of course, they were tall, athletic, and popular, and I seemed to be their exact opposite in every way. My dad noticed that I was struggling, and he helped me channel what I was going through into working out; he really took me under his wing during a difficult time. I remember watching *Pumping Iron* with him, and deciding that I wanted to get into bodybuilding.

Everyone rooted for Lou Ferrigno, Franco Columbu, or Mike Katz because they were the underdogs. But not me—as soon as I saw Arnold Schwarzenegger, I just knew he was a winner. He had this confidence, this swagger about him, that was magical to a kid like me. And of course the ladies were crazy about him, whereas I couldn't repel them fast enough. I became a little obsessed with emulating him. In the documentary, Arnold said that the bodybuilder is an artist and a sculptor; he sculpts his body to perfection, adding and subtracting necessary pieces in order to reach the ideal. He said that it was important to work methodically and tirelessly, and to devote yourself to the goal. And I took that really seriously. I didn't want to be the underdog, the loser; I wanted to be a winner.

In some ways, discovering bodybuilding was good because it helped me take control of my life. I felt less like a victim and more like I could fight back. I started working out every day, twice a day. Gradually, I started getting bigger and bigger, and my confidence really skyrocketed. I stopped getting picked on. I started eating more carefully, working out more strategically, and my body was responding. I could control everything it did, and there was something exhilarating about that control—you know, when everything else is falling apart, you can go work out and you know exactly what to expect. Like Arnold said, I was sculpting my aesthetic. Eventually, once it became a lifestyle, I started competing and placing.

But at some point along the road, I found out that I'd tied my self-worth to my body shape. Whenever I don't do well in competi-

tions, I punish myself. I did, and still do, a lot of unhealthy and un-
natural things. I take steroids, I take supplements, I take diuretics;
I've made myself throw up. I've gone on every diet you can think
of—keto, counting macros, vegan, etc. I haven't had water in over a
day to water-deplete before a competition. I weigh my food. Every
Sunday, I plan my meals for the week, and I batch cook them so
that I'm never tempted to deviate. I haven't had a cheat meal in
years (one that's not being filmed for YouTube, that is), and when I
go off my meal plan even slightly, I go to the gym for hours. I am hy-
percritical of myself. Once a week, I get naked and mark myself up
in front of the mirror like a plastic surgeon might so that I know
what I need to work on.

All of this makes it hard to get close to someone, so I haven't
really ever had a serious relationship. The only person who really
knows what it's like to live a day in my life is me, and that's really
isolating. But there's also a little bit of comfort in the distance and
the discipline. I know that I don't ever really have to worry about
judgment in a way that would truly hurt because I keep myself so
hidden. Having everything so rigidly planned gets rid of uncomfortable gray areas; it makes me feel that, ultimately, I am the master of
my fate.

My last relationship ended because I couldn't let her see "the
real me": the physical and psychological punishment, the grueling
workouts, the bullshit social media posts, the image obsession.
There was always a polite distance between our lives, and she
started to sense it. She started to ask questions: "Do you want kids?
Where do you see us going? What are your plans for the future?"
There's only so long that you can sidestep questions like those. The
more I'd avoid them, the more direct she became. We were driving
on the highway one day, on our way home from visiting her older
sister. Every time we'd visit, she'd see the baby, I guess, and feel
pressure to also move her life forward. So she started up with the
questions again, and I lost my cool. I started yelling at her and almost lost control of the car. I remember I was banging my hand on

the steering wheel, and I guess the horn was going off because cars were passing by, looking at us. She broke up with me after that. Over text. Can't say I blame her.

Most people don't see that side of my life, though. They see what I post online, and they assume, *Here's this attractive guy with thousands of followers, he must be really killing it.* The whole thing is for show, even the muscles. Even though I shouldn't take anything that's said online personally because I know it's not real, I'm still human. The impersonal nature of an influencer's public Instagram account makes people think that they can say anything and pick a person apart without any repercussions. I've gotten all sorts of vicious comments about my body, my intelligence, and my manhood (a favorite topic of discussion). Of course, I'm sitting on the other side of that screen, reading every comment and taking it to heart.

The thing is, you build a following by engaging with your audience and you start to kind of get to know the people who are always liking and commenting. People get really demanding and nosy—if you miss a post, your DMs are getting blown up. When my girlfriend and I broke up, people noticed almost immediately that I wasn't posting photos of us anymore—they wanted to know what had happened. I'm putting my life out there willingly, so it's not like I'm expecting privacy, but it can really become overwhelming sometimes, like a pseudo celebrity. Whether you like it or not, people also start to idolize you. A lot of my followers are younger, and that makes me feel kind of guilty. I'm responsible in what I post—even though I use unhealthy methods to achieve my look, it's not something I am open about on Instagram—but I am afraid that I am portraying an unattainable aesthetic to young people.

I guess I would say, to anyone looking at my account online, to not be distracted by people who put up "real" unposed photos in order to humanize themselves and make you feel that you're just like them. Don't—for a second—think that just because someone seems "no-nonsense," he or she wouldn't try to sell you a weight-loss tea or a vitamin that won't do anything for you but will make them thousands of dollars. It's all smoke and mirrors. It's all a business—the business of selling one's image.

But at the end of the day, anyone going to the gym as much as the people in the Instagram fitness community do is not healthy; there's no balance in that lifestyle. It's an obsession. Maybe someone else's obsession is money, or fame, or validation. But whatever it is, eventually it all comes crashing down. My obsession is control. If I can control my body, I can control something. What worries me is the long-term repercussions. I can't bring myself to think about how much damage I've done to my health.

Psychologically, I am so messed up. I am still that little kid who wanted to be loved and accepted—who never was. It's aggravating to me that someone like me, who thrives on control and order, can't seem to get a handle on something that happened such a long time ago. It's just so hard to address because a lot of it has crusted over already and I don't feel like picking at it. So instead, I've put on these layers of armor to protect myself from other people—the muscles, the lifestyle, the whole image—and nobody's ever really gotten to know the real me. I'm not even sure I remember who that is anymore because I've put on blinders and told myself that this is what I need to do to be happy, so now there's no turning back.

I see the likes pile up on Instagram, and it's this shallow gratification because I know it's not even really me they're liking, but I still sit there and watch the notifications. They're liking someone I've created, and I guess there's still some pride in that. It's exactly like a drug: it's beyond logic. I know that as soon as it wears off, I'll be back in the real world. But it feels so good while it lasts, so why not just let it run? And then, as soon as the likes slow down, I'm thinking about the next post, the next pose, the next challenge. If I stopped doing it, I would be nobody. I have to buy into it now; it's too late. If the cracks show, people sense it. Especially online, people are vicious; they're unforgiving.

Ben, early thirties

One of the central roads in Pristina runs right behind my apartment building, and I stood on the balcony that night and watched rows of tanks pass by. I was twelve years old. We were watching BBC in our living room a couple of weeks before, and the news anchor was reporting that Serbs were taking Kosovar families out of houses in the villages and killing them. Women and children, too. And I remember thinking, *Why would they kill women and children?* A few days later, there were violent demonstrations in Pristina and I watched on TV as the Serbian police forces beat protesters.

Soon after, the news became saturated with stories about violence in the smaller villages in Kosovo. Our classes in school started filling up with displaced children from those villages. They spoke Albanian, but with thicker accents. I remember the OSCE [the Organization for Security and Co-operation in Europe] had sent a mission to Kosovo to observe the situation, and they left. Slowly but surely, over a few weeks, most of the other foreigners left, too, and then everyone who had a car or could take a bus went to Albania, Macedonia, or Montenegro, to live in refugee camps. But we were stuck in Kosovo. And that's when things got really scary.

My mom, my four siblings, and I lived on the top floor of a three-story apartment building. When the NATO bombing started in 1999, the occupants of the second and third floor all moved down to the first-floor apartment—there were twenty-two of us altogether who slept there at night in order to avoid danger from possible air strikes. Actually, I don't even know if we slept, because it would have been impossible, space-wise. We blanketed the windows of all the rooms so that there were no lights visible from the outside. We could feel the windows shaking, which is how we knew that the bombing was close by. Each morning after, we would listen to the radio to keep informed about what was happening—where the skirmishes had been, how many had died. This went on for seventy-eight days.

School was canceled, so we kids were sometimes allowed to play outside during the day. When the sirens signaling an impending attack would go off, we'd all rush inside. The phones were disconnected, so we couldn't communicate with family. My whole extended family was kicked out and sent to a refugee camp in Albania, and we didn't even know about it until the war ended. I remember that the stores were closed, too, but sometimes they would open for a few hours and people would have to wait in line for necessities—bread, milk, cheese.

Every day, we saw pictures of dead people on TV. One evening, we could see shooting—the lights from the gunfire—very close to my building. My mother was losing her mind with worry because my brother wasn't home, and she was afraid he might get caught in the cross fire. Thankfully, he got home later that night, but we found out the next day that an Albanian journalist had been ambushed by the Serbs and killed. Until then, all the violence had been in the villages, but if you are aware that destruction is happening everywhere, you accept that it will eventually reach you, too.

As I understand it, the problem between Kosovo and Serbia started in 1989. Kosovo was an autonomous region of Serbia, but when Milošević, the new Serbian president, took power, he rescinded autonomy. He fired Kosovars from well-paying jobs and encouraged Serbians to move to Kosovo to replace them. There were no TV channels in Albanian, and if you had to do anything official, you had to communicate in Serbian. Even though Serbians were a minority in Kosovo, they ran everything. In schools, there was a separate entrance and separate classrooms for Serbian kids. Their part of the school was *much* nicer.

A few Serbian families lived in my neighborhood, but for the most part they kept to themselves. Because we didn't intermingle and didn't speak the same language, there were never any instances of violence between us. The only really bad interaction with a Serbian that I remember was when this Albanian kid actually threw a rock at my sister. She ducked, though, and it hit me on the forehead. There was a lot of blood, and I was crying. We went to the ER to get stitches, and of course all the doctors and nurses were Serbian. They stitched my forehead up without anesthesia, and I was shouting and crying from pain. My mother—her generation had to learn Serbian in school—understood what they had been saying and translated for me when I asked her many years later. The gist of the sentiment had been something along the lines of "See, there's something wrong with these people. They're animals."

The kid's mom came over and apologized for what her son had done. I still have the scar on my forehead.

Overall, I think about thirteen thousand Kosovars died during the war. During the seventy-eight days of bombing, the Serbian military would go into the buildings and check every apartment. In some places, they took adult men and killed them, presumably to keep them from joining the Kosovo Liberation Army. They checked our apartment and even though I was very afraid, the three soldiers left without hurting us.

Another almost 900,000 people were displaced. We didn't leave because, actually, my dad died one month before the war in Kosovo started. We were shocked and grieving his death, so there just wasn't enough time to mobilize. My mom must have also been afraid to pick up five kids and move them on her own.

My dad worked a lot. He was an economist. On the weekends, he cooked. For a long time, my mom kept a bag of letters that he wrote her when they were dating. I don't really have very many other memories of him. His death was unexpected. He started to feel unwell, and I remember that he went to the hospital. They kept him overnight to monitor him and do some tests. And then I guess a neighbor knew someone who worked at the hospital, and she came over and told us that my dad had died. I remember my mom crying and being pretty devastated. I cried, too. We went from one tragedy to the next.

One morning in June 1999, we woke up really early and we could see military vehicles from NATO in the streets of Pristina. We were so happy. It meant the war was over. All the kids went to the side of the road and started applauding the British troops. Some people even gave them flowers, and they would give us sweets. I don't remember what they were called but they were very colorful. I liked the candy, but mostly I was excited because it was the first time I'd met people for whom English was a native language and I wanted to practice speaking with them.

Two years later, in 2001, one of my teachers in school told me about a program that brought together people from areas of conflict and tried to engender dialogue between them. The program included a summerlong stay at a camp in the United States. To be honest, all I cared about at the time was that it was an opportunity to visit the US. I applied, and sometime later, I remember getting mail telling me that I was one of the four people accepted into the program. I couldn't believe that it was actually happening because America was just something I saw on TV. But the next thing I knew, I had an appointment for a visa, and then a couple of days later, I was headed to the airport. We flew from Kosovo to Switzerland, then to Austria, where we had to stay overnight. I wound up having to share a bed with one of the Serbian kids. It was very awkward. The next day, we flew to Boston. And from Boston we drove to the camp.

We arrived there at night, after curfew. All the lights were off. We entered the cabins with lamps, and to me it seemed so unpleasant. And I said to myself, *Why did I come to America?* I woke up the next day, and there were so many activities that I didn't have time to breathe. At the end of the three weeks, I realized that everyone is the same—a human being taught a different version of history.

While I was at camp, one of the staff members had arranged for an admissions counselor from Goucher College to speak to us. I remember getting the idea that it's possible to study in the US even if you don't have any money. If you're lucky, you can get a scholarship. I remember looking up what I'd have to do—take the TOEFL [Test of English as a Foreign Language] for non-native English speakers, and then the SAT. On the last day of camp, the counselors took us to a local mall. One of them, an American guy I'd really bonded with, bought me an SAT book as a present.

He said, "So if you want to come to the US, this is what you have to study." I think I still have that book somewhere—it's pretty marked up.

I went back to Kosovo and applied to a bunch of schools abroad—some in Switzerland, but most in the US. I picked where to go on the basis of which city I wanted to visit, so I ended up in New York. I was so excited about studying in the States that I didn't think about all the details. I took two pieces of luggage in which I fit my whole life, and when I got to my dorm room, I realized I didn't have sheets for my bed. It was late, 7:00 or 8:00 p.m., so I couldn't even go out to buy any. I slept on the bare mattress, and I remember it was so hard. On the second day, the school organized a trip to Target for international students. I had some money, and I bought the necessities, but I couldn't afford a computer. I actually didn't own a laptop until the end of sophomore year. I used the library computers to do my work. The first semester was hard because I needed to have a 3.2 GPA to keep my scholarship, and I'd never had a class in English, so I studied constantly. But I finished college with a 3.99 GPA. The only A- I got was in an English writing class I took freshman year.

During my senior year, I realized I was pretty good at math. I decided to apply to a few math PhD programs, and once again, I picked the program on the basis of which city I wanted to visit. This time, I ended up in DC. My mom even made it to my hooding ceremony, which was really great, since she was denied a visa when she tried to come for my undergraduate graduation ceremony. I could tell she was really proud of me, but she complained a lot about the food here.

Now I am a math professor at one of the best universities in the country. I think back on how I got here, against some crazy odds. I guess who makes it in this life depends a lot on pure luck, and I have to admit that I've been very lucky. But it also matters how hard you're willing to work and persevere. Life is difficult. It's one of those things that I didn't take time to think about much—I just kept going. I was surviving.

Gordon, forties

We were in his father's toolshed, in the backyard. The door was closed. I was probably six. He was nine or ten. We'd been doing this for a while—a few months, maybe almost a year. We were just being curious and learning about our bodies—touching, nothing more serious than that.

My mom came in, and then his mom, and I remember a lot of commotion and shouting as they jumped on us and pulled us apart. My mom rushed me back home, and she told my dad. I don't know how he took it, because I wasn't in the room at the time, but I was never allowed to go back and my friendship ended. My parents also ended all contact with the young boy's family. I had no idea that what I was doing—and whom I was doing it with—was a problem. It wasn't until I witnessed my mother's reaction, and then it was impressed upon me continuously by my religion—the Mormon faith—that this was a sin, an abomination, that I realized I had done something bad and that I should be ashamed of myself. My parents called it "a form of molestation." I thought we were just being kids, doing what came naturally.

I was so traumatized by what happened and my parents' reaction that I didn't do anything again until I hit puberty, so when I was about eleven or twelve. This time, it was with another childhood friend, and it brought my sexuality back to the forefront.

My mom's side of the family is Baptist and Lutheran. It's my dad's side, the Mormon side, that's very religious. Our religion was a thread that ran through my whole childhood—everything that I did. The church made it absolutely clear that my homosexuality was a choice, and in being gay, I chose to commit a sin. And thus began my double life. Publicly, I was a good Mormon. Privately, I was just like any other teenager: I wanted to explore my sexuality. Counteracting this period of self-exploration was also a tremendous amount of guilt, shame, and remorse. I was often in tears because I couldn't understand my feelings. Homosexuality was shunned in the church and in our community, so I felt like I was the only one going through this, even though I'm certain I wasn't. I was too petrified to talk to anyone else, though. Interacting with peers was difficult because I was not confident and comfortable in my own skin. I didn't know if it was okay to be myself. In fact, I was certain it was not okay to be myself.

In my experience, the Mormon Church has a really effective way of reinforcing their core beliefs. Starting at age twelve, I had to sit in front of a church authority figure we called "the bishop," and he would ask me a list of questions. I remember he asked me if I had impure thoughts and if I masturbated. And I had to tell him the things I'd done and the things I'd thought. I remember being so worried that he'd tell my parents or other members of the church, and so I learned to lie to his face. I couldn't tell him what I was actually thinking, and I couldn't tell him that I wasn't thinking anything at all—yeah, right, who would believe that from a twelve-year-old?—so I just made the most mundane things up: "I fantasize about kissing a girl."

At age fourteen, I lost my virginity. It was not traumatic for me at all. It was a very good experience, and it happened at the right time because I was maturing quickly. It was with a close friend of mine from school. He brought up the idea of maybe going all the way. We were both nervous about it, so we kept it 100 percent between us. I was in a steady sexual relationship with him for two years. We would go to his house after school—his parents and brother were working, so we spent time alone almost every day. All these experiences, all together, were positive reinforcements that I was gay.

At age nineteen, I went on a two-year church mission in Europe. I was in constant fear of acting out my feelings and the consequences that would follow, so I stayed completely celibate. I thought that because I was "good," that I would be "normal" when I got back. When I finished my mission, I thought to myself that things were resolved. But I went to college for a short time, and I found that I still had tendencies. I felt like a failure because I was hoping that I was healed and I could live my life the way I was taught I should. Being in college just made it clear that I couldn't fight the temptation. So college didn't pan out. I picked a vocation and finished school in that field, and then I got really lucky and was offered an opportunity to go back to Europe and work there for a while.

That was the turning point for me. Even though I was only there for two months, I got really close to the staff and I told them that I was gay. There were other gay people there (also Mormons), and they took me out and showed me around. I got to experience the nightlife. Things are a lot more liberal in Europe than they are in the States. Nobody looked or judged. I could be who I wanted to be, and that gave me the distance I needed for perspective. Europe, the second time around, gave me the chance to detach from the church and learn about myself. Those two months saved my life.

When I came back, I decided to see a therapist. I guess I rationalized it as one last attempt to cure myself, to get healed, to overcome the gay—I had read online that there were people who could do this. A bigger part of me, though, hoped that he would offer some guidance in learning to accept myself. Thankfully, he was a totally no-BS kind of guy and he very kindly said, "Look, this is who you are. There's nothing wrong with you. I'm going to help you see that."

I started to see that regardless of what I had been taught my whole life, I needed to stop treating myself like a problem. I needed to stop hiding from myself. It was a long road to acceptance, and I encountered a lot of challenges, a lot of people who at times made me hate who I was. But I also had a lot of blessings—a lot of other people who drowned out the hatred with their kindness, who held my hand and gave me the space that I needed to become confident in myself.

When I felt ready to tell my family, my father tragically and unexpectedly passed away. As the oldest of the kids, I was suddenly thrust into this position of having to be the "man of the house." It just didn't feel like a good time to tell everyone. Three years after his death, I came out to my sister. She's five years younger, and I had a feeling that she would be the most sympathetic. She was very kind and accepting, and she helped me tell the rest of the family. My mother cried, but I think she always knew, so she accepted it. I have close to one hundred cousins on my dad's side of the family alone. None of them talk to me anymore. All my dad's family turned their backs on me. I think they probably would feel like traitors to the family and the church if they accepted me.

But I have a lot of family who cares for me and whose opinion of me hasn't changed. I think my father would have been one of them—he would have accepted me. So I feel a lot of sadness that I never got to tell him before he died. People think, *Oh, that won't happen to me*—no one is ever prepared to lose a parent—but you never know what could happen. It took a long time for it to hit me that he died, for my brain to catch up with the reality. It wasn't until four months later that I broke down and cried because something reminded me of him.

When my father passed away, most of my close family also broke away from the Mormon Church. I am not so much Mormon anymore. I don't really hold any hard feelings against the church for the way that I was treated. I think people do what they know, and many of them never question what they're taught. They live their whole lives never moving too far away from the home in which they were raised, never having occasion to question the truths that someone else hands them, fearing that they'll end up on the outside of this very tight-knit circle of people. I feared the outside, too. There's so much comfort in being one with others. In the church, people bring you food when you're sick, they pick up the slack when you need help, they really look out for one another. It's one big, extended family. And when your family and identity and everything you've ever known depend on being accepted by the church, the outside of that circle is a scary place to be. So choosing to honor this part of myself meant accepting that I might lose another part of my identity. Maybe not lose—maybe it's more accurate to say that I might be kicked out of another part of my identity. That was very difficult. But my choice caused me to question everything, to really expand my horizons—to find things out for myself. Life is so much fuller, so much truer, so much more beautiful because of it.

If there's an aspect of my Mormon religion that has stuck with me, it's the importance of family—and the idea that the family unit stays together forever. This past November, I married a wonderful man. I look forward to building a family with him. I am lucky in many ways because I made it through the hard times, but I know there are a lot of kids out there who are struggling and who think they are alone. I remember being in their shoes, and I remember how much I needed someone to tell me that there was nothing wrong with me—that I was not a sin, or an abomination, or a shameful person—and so I guess I just want them to know that it will be okay.

Steve, late sixties

Author's note: I have tried to stay faithful to the flow of conversation with Steve, and, as a result, some passages may be unclear.

What I think changes all the time. It goes to different thoughts.

Different. My life has been different. Because of how dumb my mother and father were. And how dumb the doctors were in my generation. They couldn't connect the dots on what was wrong with me. The doctor was cold. The way he talked to me scared me.

I was shy as a kid. I lived with my family of six in a small house, and I would cry all the time when I wasn't picked up. Until my brother hit me in the head with a baseball bat when I was five years old. And that's when things went sideways. I started worrying that people were looking at me through the windows of our house. . . .

In school, nobody wanted to play with me. Nobody wanted to talk to me. It's because I had these glasses. All the other kids were wearing plastic glasses. My doctor had this one pair of glasses and he stuck them on me. They had a metal rim. They were different, and so they made me *feel* different. My glasses were silver and black. They made me feel ugly. They made me have low self-worth. And so I was depressed.

My brother—I have a younger brother—we went to summer camp together. I was twelve, maybe. And my brother wouldn't talk to me. My mother told me that I would have to look after him, but I left him, and he never forgave me. I saw him three weeks ago for the first time in twenty-two years. Three weeks ago, our father died. We were at his funeral. He was ninety-five.

Our mother is eighty-nine. She always put our father down at dinnertime because he had dyslexia. My mother is on the Facebook. She's an artist. She is really into her art but not so much into her kids. She's the type of woman who glorifies other women. My brother took fifteen years to get through school; he got a PhD. He was married, but he divorced her because she gained weight and she got too big. He was at the funeral with his new girlfriend. He has become a playboy, and his ex-wife still loves him. He's a creep. Unique, over-the-top kind of guy.

I could never talk to girls when I was in school. Couldn't trust them. I never had a girlfriend until I was thirty-three. I thought to myself, *Oh, I guess she likes me.*

I had a hard time as a baby. It was a cesarean birth. They used the forceps to pull me out. It crushed my head a little bit.

Suicide is constantly a threat to me. When my uncle is gone, I don't know how I'll pay the bills. Maybe I could find another old guy that I could live with and I would make his life better because I have lots of room to care for other people. I work a little bit here and there, but it's hard to run a business. I painted my truck all different colors. People don't like different.

I took LSD when I was in college. I tried college for one year. We smoked pot and drank. I went into stores and thought I was going to die. LSD made me feel normal the first time I took it. But afterward, it messed me up worse. I was 115 pounds. I couldn't eat. The doctors were crazy! So now I'm addicted to the medication. I can't get off it.

Where I live now, I live with my uncle because he needs someone to take care of him. He's old. They don't like different here. Back when I lived in Arizona, they went after me because rumor started that I was more expensive than everyone else. Everyone chimed in, and that's what I became. . . . But here, nobody knows that I'm a decent person. No matter what I do, I am wrong. They inflict pain on people who don't fit. It's one of these small towns that stick together even when they're wrong.

I went into Walmart one day, and all the ladies who work there were lined up behind the cash register and they were looking at me, they were staring at me. At one time, I thought that everyone was staring at me. I was looking at them for approval.

It is a crime of society that I never got treatment until I was thirty-four. I don't look at faces and eyes anymore; I glance over their heads. "There's that guy that stares at everyone," they say. There's dead silence, and everyone is staring at me. They spread the rumor at Walmart and Home Depot and Lowe's. They want to hurt me so that I can't approach women. Because I'm from the wrong side of the tracks. Black ladies think I'm pretty cool, and I like them all right, too.

I run my own business. I am a handyman, and I charge very reasonable prices. I'm good with my hands. I have my own truck.

People lie to me constantly. I was attacked twenty years ago. I have a fear of being attacked again. I am also afraid of people in groups. And I'm afraid people in groups will attack me.

My medication hurts me sometimes. I have never had an orgasm. My girlfriend is 275 pounds.

They put me on Nardil. It's one of the first antidepressants. It came out in the sixties. When I tried to get off it, I got suicidal. It consumed my thoughts. I wanted to get off the medication for a long time. It made it so that I can't communicate with people. I was in a group for anxiety. If you looked at people in the eye, they would feel bothered.

I am very lonely. I want to talk to people, but they don't like me. They watch me when I'm not paying attention. I have a genetic predisposition to anxiety, but my brother says that I am delusional. He tried to tell me at the funeral that I need help, but I am okay. I am perfectly fine. I'm different, and people don't like different. I didn't get any help until I was thirty-four, and even then the doctors just wanted to put me on drugs. I want to feel good about me, I don't want drugs.

I can't work now because people say I charge unfair prices, so my business went under. My uncle gets some money from his pension, and we live together. When I was going to buy materials for work, people at the stores were whispering behind my back. It was dead silent except for their whispers. And they were saying, "There's that guy that overcharges."

"There's that guy with the truck."

"There's that guy who is always staring at people."

I try to set people at ease that I'm a good guy. I look just above their faces, and I smile at them.

My father was an Eagle Scout. He was very difficult to communicate with, and my brother is impossible to communicate with. I hate my mother. I think I was molested as an infant. But she doesn't care. She cares about her art, and that's it. People are not good. This world is not good. I used to think that the world was an okay place, but that happened until I was in grade school. So the world is definitely not good, and people cannot be trusted.

I try to be helpful even though I can't work. I don't like living off people. My brother doesn't like me living with my uncle because he thinks I'll inherit everything and my brother won't get anything. I help my uncle take his medication, and I keep him company. I change his sheets, and I help him wash up when he needs it. And I go out and do the shopping for us. I don't like to do it, but I do. My uncle understands me. He's not like my parents, who moved into a retirement community and only care about themselves. He cares about me. I will be sad when he dies, but maybe I can find another old person. . . .

I don't want to talk about it. I like talking to people but not about what happened. I think it happened when I was a newborn.

I try to find people to be friends with, but it's difficult to control my emotions.

I can look back now, and it doesn't hurt in the same way. I am glad I never actually tried to kill myself.

I keep trying. I always looked at my life as climbing a mountain, where I slipped and fell down the mountain. I tried to get over an agoraphobic existence for thirty years. You feel sick when you eat, go anywhere, or do anything. I got over that at fifty-eight and then was further humiliated by bigots in their small world. They were taunting me with "He stares at everyone." The people here showed how small people can be with their small-town attitudes that made no sense to anyone outside this area. All this was to show others how powerful they were while I can only feel sorry for all of them.

I tried to wash windows to make money, but after ten years someone started a rumor I was a rip-off with my prices.

That was another mountain I had to climb after winning my inner battle at fifty-eight with agoraphobia. I had to be strong enough to stand up to the idiots giving me dirty looks and talking to other people when I was in a store about how I was this person no one liked. I got back up and started climbing again. Things have settled down after the first years of this dilemma. I now wish to meet other people, and I may have to relocate to do this. Another mountain to climb, because I know I could fail again.

It only takes me to make a few mistakes and things start to unwind pretty quickly.

It's a man's world; the male is the one looked at as the evil one, and the woman is usually looked at with much more empathy by both sexes. I do know that in society, men are more the evil ones to other men and women. In my case, to hang any negative slant on my existence has been easy for others to do even if it isn't true.

I lived with an uncle at the time, and to celebrate my anxiety getting better, we started to go to a local restaurant where I felt happy to look around the room at different women, married or single. I noticed that they didn't like that too much because they started talking among themselves about me.

I told my uncle I don't think we should go there anymore. He said he had to have the salmon dinner each week, so I said okay reluctantly.

The last time we went there, there were three people waiting for us at the car. My ninety-year-old uncle got so nervous that as soon as he got in the car, he said he never wanted to go back there again. I told him it was a little too late for him to understand this.

Yes, it is sad.

FAMILY

Lee, early fifties

I was a scrawny kid with thin, little matchstick legs that stuck out of my shorts. My mother combed my hair carefully every morning before school. She always smelled sweet—like fully bloomed roses in the peak of their beauty—and I cherished the few seconds before the bus rounded the corner when she would touch my shoulder and hand me my lunch box. She never touched me or showed much affection otherwise, so those few moments of closeness shocked my body, and I felt in high spirits all day.

I was eleven when it started, just before my father died. My cousin Joe came over every day that summer, and we would spend hours running around and causing trouble. When the sun started to hover over the horizon and I could see the heat rising from the asphalt in ripples, I knew that any minute, my mother would call us in for dinner. The anticipation of the end of the day made my chest swell with a mix of sadness that it was over and excitement that we'd get to do it all over again the next day.

These are the only days that I felt truly, simply happy. I was sticky and tired, my knees were scraped up and bloody, and my clothes torn in more places than my mother could patch up. But that summer serves as my only reminder that I was once a child, and that things weren't always so hard, so complicated.

On that particular night, Joe and I took turns showering while my mom and uncle, my mother's brother, set the table. I was voracious, and my eating was punctuated only by spontaneous giggles. My cousin would shoot me mischievous looks over his plate of pasta, and we both reveled in the memories of the day's adventures.

When it was time to sleep, I let my full stomach weigh me down onto the clean linens of my childhood bed. I felt just the right amount of tired, and my body relaxed into the thin mattress as I relished the way that the sheets covered my legs with their cucumber coolness. If I remember these moments, these sensations, so clearly, it's because I've spent many a sleepless night wishing that I could freeze time here.

I was slowly drifting to sleep when my uncle pushed open the creaky bedroom door.

He sat by Joe's bed and started whispering in his ear. I couldn't hear what he was saying, and I strained to make out the words. I hated being left out of conversations, and the tone of my uncle's voice made me feel like I was the only one not in on the secret. But the more my eyes tried to peripherally pick up on what was happening, the more I felt a sense of foreboding in the pit of my stomach. The situation felt predatory, like I'd just walked in on a lion stalking his kill and, if I made myself known, I'd somehow put a target on my own back. I gave up trying to hear after a while, allowing the rhythmic sandpapery sound of my uncle's hand as it rubbed Joe's chest lull me into a shallow calm. I hovered there for maybe ten minutes.

Suddenly, I sensed movement, and I cracked my eyes open just slightly to assess the source. My uncle walked across the room slowly and sat on the edge of my bed. I kept my eyes shut, and tried to steady my breathing, but I felt inexplicably panicked. I knew immediately that I was in danger. Even though my experience with sex was limited to the summer before, when I'd summoned up the courage to look at the lingerie section of the Sears catalog, I just knew that something bad or shameful was going to happen, or maybe had already happened.

For no reason that I could understand then, I started crying, quietly at first. My uncle tried to comfort me, telling me that he wasn't doing anything wrong or bad, that it was natural, that it would be our secret. He mentioned nothing specific, but I knew what he was referring to—maybe a part of me had always felt that it was weird that he'd come into our room and sat on Joe's bed for so long.

My sobs got louder, and my uncle got up and stood watchfully over us for a moment's time. Then he did something that I just didn't understand: he picked Joe up and he put him on my bed but over my sheets, our bodies overlapping slightly on the twin mattress. Then he swiftly walked out of the room. I finally looked at Joe, who was motionless and seemed to have stopped breathing altogether. His expression was one of fixed terror, and even his tears seemed to be petrified on his sad little face.

As if roused from a daze, he carefully peeled himself off my bed and robotically, limb by limb, scooted under my sheets. We held hands the whole night. I could hear my cousin crying well into midnight, but my own confusion kept me awake and struggling to understand what had happened, what it meant. I know now that my uncle was planting a seed for the future. He was grooming me.

After my father died, my uncle started coming over every week, or he'd invite me over to his house under the pretext of being a "father figure." Joe would come up to me and say, "My dad wants to see us." My uncle would usually start out by talking to us about sports or whatever else, and then eventually Joe would leave and I'd be there by myself. He usually gave me oral sex. He'd try to get me to do things, too, but I'd just freeze up my body so that he couldn't move me. It didn't happen very often, actually—probably only five or six times in the span of two years. I don't remember why it stopped. It just did.

Needless to say, as an adult I have a very unhealthy relationship with sex. I am addicted to pornography, and I have cheated on my wife about a dozen times throughout our marriage—a couple of women over an extended period of time. My wife found some porn on my computer. This was long before the days when you could just go on a website and clear your history; I had downloaded all the stuff I was watching. So she started asking questions, and I just came out with all of it, told her everything. I wanted affirmation from her—but I think she thought I was just using my past as an excuse for my current behavior. There was also rumor, and I found this out long after I'd married her, that her father, who was a gymnastics coach, had abused his students. So maybe she just wanted no part of it.

I found no understanding in her, no healing for my wounds. We have three daughters—the eldest is twenty-one. Once we decided to divorce, my wife made me sit down and tell the children about the affairs and the pornography. And about the abuse. So they all know. They weren't supposed to, and I didn't agree to tell them. My wife, however, needed to be vindicated. She needed to feel that leaving me was the right thing, and that I was a cheater who had broken our marriage.

Telling my daughters was the wrong thing to do, and it felt dehumanizing. I've always thought that as a parent, I had to have it all together, or at least seem like I did; I had to be the adult they trusted with their problems. But the looks on their faces betrayed that something was lost between us. It was a cross between disgust and bewilderment. My wife led the narrative, so, of course, the focus was on the cheating and the porn addiction, and the childhood trauma was an afterthought. At the end, I could tell that they saw me differently, I could just tell. I don't think it would have mattered to me if their reaction had been one of sympathy, although I did hope that what happened to me as a child would soften their judgment. But it's not their end of the equation that mattered so much as mine. My perception of myself as a father just didn't survive this revelation.

I had lost touch with Joe after we graduated from high school. I spent a lot of time wondering what had happened to him. And then, four years ago, I found out that he had filed a civil suit against my uncle for the sexual abuse. He reached out to me to get me involved, and I was really unsure about it. I was going through so much with my own family, and the last thing I wanted to do was make things worse. But it did bring about an opportunity to talk to my mom about what had happened, to finally tell her about what her brother had done.

I thought she would be surprised. I thought that maybe she might cry, even though she was never a crier. I thought she would be angry and ask questions. I thought that she would blame herself, and I imagined myself saying, "No, there was no way you could have known." I thought she might want to know how long it went on for, to which I would say, "Only a few times." I thought that she would try to reach her brother, to threaten him with death and serious bodily injury. I thought that she might even touch my shoulder like she used to, as we waited for the bus together. I thought she might hug me and apologize for not being more suspicious, more watchful, more careful.

She did none of those things. I watched her face for her reaction, and I waited for her to say something, anything, about what I'd just revealed. But I realized that that was it—her reaction. Nothing. It dawned on me that she had known. Of course she had known.

Sylvie, late forties

I've seen my son, Alex, twice since the divorce five years ago. Once, for his high school graduation; the other, when I pulled up to my ex-husband Evan's house to drop off Anna, our younger daughter. Alex was mowing the lawn. He saw my Volvo round the corner, and he ran into the house. His reaction was visceral, knee-jerk, like he'd seen a snake in the grass. To see my son respond like that tore my heart apart.

When things went south, Evan wanted to work on our marriage. At the time, I didn't. We were high school sweethearts, married for over twenty years. We had started growing apart over the last few years of our marriage. My mother-in-law was part of the problem; she was really controlling and would habitually show up unannounced. She drove a wedge in our marriage, likely because her own was failing. But it's unfair to put it all on her: we were struggling and had been for a while. We weren't communicating well—or at all, really. We didn't spend any quality time together; physical intimacy was nonexistent. Really, we'd become strangers who were living together and happened to share children.

I was a good wife right until the very end. We were fighting a lot, my ex and I. The kids knew it, too. Alex was old enough to understand; Anna was on the cusp. We were on a family trip when my phone lit up. It was a Facebook friend request notification from Brad, my first love when I was a kid. I hadn't seen him or heard from him in decades. I told Evan about it, and he said he didn't care if I spoke to him, which was kind of typical of him, to be so aloof. So I accepted the request. And you know how these things happen—one thing leads to another.

We were getting ready to sit down to dinner one night. I had been having an affair with Brad for three months by then. I think I was at the sink, washing lettuce for the salad. My phone kept ringing and ringing, but my hands were wet, so I didn't pick it up. My sister was visiting, and she said something like, "Hey, why aren't you picking it up?" Of course, Evan picked up the phone, and that was that. In retrospect, I was being so reckless that part of me thinks I wanted to be found out.

Up to that point, things had been going well with Brad. I was excited by how new and good it was. When everything blew up, I felt—weirdly—special. I was getting a lot of attention from both Brad and Evan. I felt wanted, worth fighting for. But I didn't have the strength to fight anymore. I wanted out of my marriage. I wanted something new and fresh—I didn't want to be married for the sake of it. I wanted romance, to feel seen, to be in love again. Should being a parent preclude that? Did I owe it to my kids to forgo a chance at my own happiness? I'm not sure I asked those questions because I wasn't thinking that I'd be found out, that it would end my marriage. It all happened very quickly.

During this time, Evan, the kids, and I all continued living together in the same house. Evan moved out of our bedroom and into the office. He became very controlling and narcissistic: everything was about him and what he did for our family—he'd run the littlest errand for the kids, something I'd been doing for years, and then mention it constantly. Or, if I wanted to do something with the kids, for example, he'd make a big deal out of it if I didn't run it by him first. It had never been like that before. I don't want to suggest that he'd been an absentee parent—he wasn't—but the kids simply didn't take up much of his time or energy. Suddenly, though, it seemed like we were in a competition for parent of the year. The tension in the house was unbearable. It felt like any one of us would go off at any second.

Our son had just started high school when the family found out about the affair, so the timing was especially bad for him. There's never a good time for your parents to divorce, but the high school years are already so precarious. We talked about it a lot with him that first week; we were trying to make sure that he was processing what had happened in a healthy way. He said that he understood, and that he didn't approve of what had happened but that he accepted it. I was so proud of him—he seemed so adult.

A month later, though, I suggested to him that we could go out to lunch with his friend and his friend's mom over school break. He said to me, "I don't want to do anything with you, ever. You're toxic, Mom. You're just toxic." The things that he was saying were things that his father would have said, things that his father had said to me—his mannerisms became similar, even. He was turning into a teenaged version of his dad. Another time, he told me, "You're sick, Mom. You need help." I confronted him about it—told him that he sounded like Evan—and he got very angry with me.

When it became clear that things wouldn't work out between me and my ex-husband, our lawyers drafted up the divorce papers. Both of us knew that things hadn't been going well between us even before the affair. Part of me thought that the kids would be relieved that the fighting was over. I remembered how awful it was for me as a child to see my parents constantly going at each other; when they separated, things got better. I always turned to that memory when I thought about my own divorce: maybe it would be better for my kids in the long run, too.

When I went in to sign the papers, I couldn't do it. I had a meltdown in my lawyer's office. I felt physically ill, confused, saddened. Because I couldn't afford to care for the kids on my own, my husband would get primary custody. I didn't feel ready to leave my family—the signature felt like my final ousting from the nest I'd helped to build for fifteen-plus years. I didn't have second thoughts because I still had feelings for Evan—I had second thoughts because of my kids. Maybe it wasn't too late to fix things for them, to minimize the damage. My lawyer called my husband's lawyer and told him I had changed my mind. I wanted to work on us.

The call back wasn't what I had expected: my ex didn't want to work it out anymore. He wanted the divorce. It felt a bit like poetic justice.

I know I made a mistake, a really big one. I shouldn't have had an affair. I should have ended our marriage decently, with a civil conversation or a nice handshake. But that's not how things played out. I'm not perfect. I feel really intense guilt about how things happened. But while I regret the circumstances, I know that I'm not just a parent. I'm a person. I need to feel loved and valued, too. I may not have always been a great wife, but I was always a great mom.

I'm afraid my kids won't remember that. I left my career behind to take care of Anna and Alex. I gave myself to them completely. And even after things ended between their father and me, I thought only about them. Maybe it was a mistake, losing myself in them. But I just never thought that my own child would hate me.

I can't understand what happened to us. I thought that Alex would get better—that maybe, with time, he would come to see that people in happy marriages don't cheat on each other. He would understand that my actions stemmed from a very deep unhappiness—and that I could not keep punishing myself for wanting to be happy again. But it got worse and worse. Every time I reached out, he screamed at me to leave him alone. Every text I sent only reopened our wounds. I can hear my ex saying the words that my son's written to me: "You had an affair with some guy while married to Dad. You acted like an insufferable psychotic jackass during the divorce process, dragging everyone down with you for nearly a year." Alex has told me that he's never had a girlfriend because of me—because he can't trust anyone.

I was watching a program on TV one night when someone said something about parental alienation, that often one parent will make the children feel that the ousted parent is either dangerous or sick. Some stranger was talking about my life—and it felt like being punched in the gut.

It seems that Evan has managed to turn Alex completely against me. He makes Alex feel that my ex is a victim and that he needs to be taken care of. I've gotten glimpses of how my ex spoke about me to Alex. While we were going through the separation, I overheard him and Alex talking one night. Alex was probably still fifteen. And my ex said to him: "Let's play a game; let's go around the room and figure out all the things your mother's going to take in the divorce." I didn't take a thing. I let my ex keep the house, and the kids stayed with him so that the disruption to their routine was minimal. They were surrounded by their things, their dog, and their friends.

Anna is different. She told me the other day, "Dad makes me feel like I have to be loyal to him." I speak to her four times a week, and she's very open with me. I can understand what it's like, being young, impressionable, rightfully angry, and wanting to make your father proud of you. It's been five years since the divorce, and parts of us have moved on, but parts of us still live with the sadness accumulated during those years. So much has changed in my life. I've gone back to school. I've started my own successful business. And I just got married—to Brad. My ex recently got engaged, too, to a woman who has a lot of money. My son is in college now. He's attending a small community school instead of the state school he'd wanted. Somehow, that also became my fault—apparently, he couldn't go because I couldn't afford to help him pay for it. The last time I spoke to him, he told me that I'd shattered our family to bits.

I sent Alex a text a little while ago. It said: "I love you, I will continue to love you, no matter what you say or how you feel."

His response: "I'm sure you will, I'm familiar with that sentiment. Now, for the final time you need to Leave. Me. Alone. That is the best thing you can do for me."

David, late fifties

I grew up on an island off the coast of South Carolina at the tail end of the civil rights era. My grandfather was a prominent figure in the civil rights movement. He was a lovely and incredibly intelligent man, even though he only had a fourth-grade education. He kept all his children and grandchildren close; we lived in an all-black community. All of us kids learned from an early age to use family as a support network because we didn't have that in society. Due to my grandfather's work, we sometimes weren't received well by our own, and definitely not by the white community, either. The white families lived separately from us, and our engagements were extremely limited. Jim Crow, de facto, was alive and well. *Is* alive and well, to some extent.

I remember as a kid we used to switch cars every day, and I thought that was really cool. I found out later that we did that to set decoys for the KKK, because they were after my grandpa. I remember hearing, too, that within a week after he took part in the bus boycott, all my grandfather's children lost their jobs. So everyone had to look for employment outside of Charleston. But that generation did this work without accolades or fanfare; they educated people. They challenged the establishment. They understood that it wasn't enough to want fair; you had to get out there and make it fair.

Now that I'm a father myself, I've become very wary of authority's response to us as black men—about the rhetoric used to advance racist agendas. I can't help the anger I feel about the things that I've witnessed over a lifetime. For instance, growing up in Low Country, I knew that there were streets, communities, and plantation properties that are named after the white families who owned us. Most people also don't know what it's like to not have their true names—my entire lineage is down in Charleston, and it goes back to three brothers who were brought there during the slave trade. Between the three of them, they all were given different names because they were bought by different families. But I don't give it any weight. I've never presented my resentments as anger; part of the reason is that the archetypal angry black man is scary to people; they're taught to fear him. Another big part is that anger, however justified, is also counterproductive.

I was talking to a friend of mine the other day, and he said to me, "We've got to stop responding like we're victims." And I understand that, but we can't deny or forget the period of time during which we were victimized. I can trace back my lineage directly to slavery. My last name isn't African—the family that owned us gave it to us. I mean, think about that: it goes back to Genesis—naming things gives you ownership over them. My family was owned.

And still today, in what is often touted as a "post-racial world," color matters. It matters even in the black community. My son went to an HBCU and he was shocked at the importance placed on being light-skinned there. People who are darker-skinned are viewed as lower—lighter-skinned black people, on the other hand, are viewed as smarter, more artistic. So are people with natural hair, or people with light eyes—any feature that's distinctive, anything that mimics white features.

At the same time, beauty ideals have changed. Twenty years ago, the curvaceous body types that are idolized now were definitely not then. Now our clothes, our hairstyles, and even our bodies are subject to cultural appropriation. But looking black stops short of *being* black—people take the parts of our identity that are convenient and fashionable, but the conversation seldom broaches how dangerous it still is to be us.

I raised my three sons on my own, and when they were growing up, I feared so much passing on that chip on the shoulder to them. Is it etched in our DNA, our past? Or is it taught to us over and over again, socialized when we're children? I was so protective of them, but I also knew that there were things I could not control. As a single parent, though, I've always felt that I had to keep them within hand's reach. So maybe I was overprotective. Maybe I protected them so much that I made the world seem kinder than it is.

My sons were raised in a predominantly white neighborhood, and a lot of our family friends are white. Not to make them wary of their white friends, I put off having the "race" conversation with them. But then they witnessed their uncle handcuffed and arrested on the pavement in front of our house—because he was parked too far away from the curb!—and I decided that this is just the reality of the world that we live in, and I could never really hide that from them. Unwarranted violence against black men is a part of our daily lives. So I told them to be careful, to realize that their skin color scares people, to not open themselves up to situations that could put them in hot water. But no matter how much I want to protect my kids, I can't change the world they live in.

One time, they had been at the mall with some friends. They were in middle school—just kids—and some cops stopped and questioned them about shoplifting. Apparently, a shopkeeper had claimed that he'd seen some black kids steal. They found nothing on them, of course, and let them go, but not before detaining them and scaring them half to death. Another time, when they were teenagers, the three of them got into a car to meet their friends at a restaurant five miles away from home. I knew their friends and where they were going. I'd done my due diligence. But they got there early, and they were sitting outside the restaurant, waiting in the parking lot, which I guess was a red flag to some people. So the police were called. That's all it takes, for people in positions of authority to say to these kids with their actions, "Hey, we see you, and this is your place in *our* society."

There is a power paradigm that tells black men to never get too comfortable in public, to never let their guard down, to never not be watching, careful, afraid, aware. Even if they aren't arrested, they're still harassed. And these are the types of things that the average black parent worries about, that just because their kids are in a group of young black men, they'll be targeted unfairly. But the cost of that is high—incredibly high. They could lose their lives.

I've always believed that if I raise my kids right, if I educate them, if I open up the world to them—that's the biggest and best thing I can do. That's the only thing I can control. My investment was in my children and in the generations to come—in posterity. I taught them to worry about their own actions and make sure they were on the straight and narrow, regardless of what happened around them. But I feel like we're traveling back in time when it comes to race relations, so I don't know if that was good advice. The only difference between now and the 1960s is that the photos are in color.

I remember the Charleston church shooting back in 2015, when Dylann Roof killed nine people in cold blood in hopes of igniting a race war. That happened in my backyard. Then, just a couple of years later, a car drove through a crowd of good people in Charlottesville, Virginia—people who were protesting against the KKK, against white supremacists who want to legitimize hatred and honor dark figures in our nation's history—figures who, had they won, would have made me and my boys slaves today. The KKK and neo-Nazis are a cancer on our society that's always been there, but the second you give them airtime, you empower them. It's disheartening, what's happening in our world today. There are so many people who aren't hard-hearted and evil, but they get caught up in this wave of demagoguery, and they become desensitized to hatred. I ask myself, *What is next?*

I can't help but think what would have happened had it been a black man who died under that car in Charlottesville. Is one life worth more than another to the media? It's a bitter pill to swallow, but precedent tells me they would have investigated him first, before reporting on the story. They would have asked: Does he have a record? They would have made him a victim twice. I've always thought that people want to sing our blues, but they don't want to live our blues.

And our president, instead of condemning racism unilaterally, got on the bully pulpit and told us that we need to preserve history and culture—that taking down pieces of history selectively is a slippery slope, and soon the likes of Washington and Jefferson will go down, too. But I have trouble seeing that: I have trouble seeing how bringing down statues that were put up during the Jim Crow and civil rights eras as a protest to black emancipation is a regressive thing for us, as a country. Shame is what's missing from our society. Shame for what was done to black people. Shame for what's still being done. I'm not worried about the men with swastika tattoos or the skinheads; I'm worried about the man walking down the street who won't look me in the eye anymore because our president has legitimized his hatred. We've allowed too much to go unchallenged.

I see *monkey* and *nigger* written on buildings now next to old murals of Barack and Michelle Obama. Having a black president was a nice symbolic gesture, but then you see messages like that and you start to wonder: How far have we *really* come?

Repression, cruelty, anger, and injustice—these things just breed more of the same unless there's a hard stop. I'm worried about my children and grandchildren; they're being robbed. Their future is being stolen from them, and their biggest loss is opportunity. So we've got to fight to make things better—all of us have to, even those who aren't directly affected. We've got to make things better. We've got to live in the blessing of today and not give any more weight to the madness of the world.

Justine, early forties

When I was in college, I remember that a girl living down the hall from me had a quote from Eleanor Roosevelt stuck on her door. It read, *A woman is like a tea bag; you can't tell how strong she is until you put her in hot water.*

Well, I come from a long line of strong tea.

My mother is an amazing woman. When she was a young girl, her parents sent her away to boarding school. My grandmother—who, by the way, is still alive and stoic as ever—had no use for babies, she used to say (and still does). She liked her kids grown, so she hired nannies to take care of them and then, once they were old enough, sent them away to school. When they came back, they were interesting young people who could match her witty banter and keep her entertained. And my mother was nothing if not entertaining. At eighteen, she ran away to Europe with a man nearly twice her age. They got married, spent a few hot months traveling around France, Italy, and Greece, and then at the end of the summer, they realized they weren't right for each other. So, without bothering to get divorced, they parted ways amicably.

The thing about my mother is that she could have made things really simple for herself. She could have lived off the family money, married well, and spent the rest of her life on vacation. But there was always something about her that, at least for me, seemed unpredictable. Even when she looked at people, she wasn't really looking at them but somewhere beyond them, like she wasn't really sure they were worth her time. She was already searching for the next best thing. So she blew off my grandmother and her life advice (of which she has plenty and gives freely) and applied to grad school in New York.

A few years later, she'd finished school and was working her way up the ranks at a big firm in the city. She went out to drinks with a girlfriend one night and met my dad. The way she told it, it was one of the few times in her life that she found it unnecessary to scan the room for someone more interesting. My father was definitely not a looker. He's aged well, but we have photos to prove that, while my mom was timelessly chic, my father seemed underwhelming next to her. He's built stocky—he jokes that it's the Italian in him (there isn't any). He's a couple of inches shorter so that, upon agreeing to go on a date with him, my mom knew that she was likely giving up one of her favorite things, her high heels, for the rest of her life. (She claimed that she was certain they would end up together.) But what he lacked in looks, my dad made up in kindness and personality. He was the life of the party, always smiling, always happy and optimistic, regardless of what was happening under the surface. He didn't come from money, and that was a novelty in the circles my mother ran in. So she was drawn to him.

His favorite story to tell us is the time that, a few months into them dating, they were walking along the water when these "three WASPs" who had been hanging out on their yacht abruptly rose to their feet and serenaded my parents with what was apparently a popular song at the time. The chorus went, "Is she really going out with him?" My dad didn't miss a beat. He dropped to his knee and asked my mother to marry him. She said yes, of course. After they'd kissed, he turned to the three men and my mother claimed he flipped them the bird.

So, that's my parents, in a nutshell.

When my grandmother met my father—on the same day they announced their engagement—apparently she immediately hated him. Their conversation was testy and high-tension, like a sideways glance might send either of them into a tailspin. I can't say that she's ever gotten over the sentiment, but my mother always did what she wanted. So after a couple of months spent hunting down her soon-to-be-ex-husband and officially procuring a divorce, my parents got married, my sister was conceived two minutes later, I was born a little over two years after her, and my brother, hot on my heels.

Growing up, I idolized my mother. She was beautiful and a little cold—she said she liked to leave people wanting more—so that my siblings and I always fought among each other for her attention and praise, both of which were in short supply. She wasn't a stay-at-home mom, which was still kind of unusual back in the 1980s, so we were raised mostly by nannies paid for by my grandmother. I know now that my grandparents were bankrolling our lifestyle. My father also worked, of course, but his career was kind of a "bonus"—although he had a solid job and made good money, his work was never really spoken about to us kids. For a long while, I wasn't even sure what he did. Whereas my mom's work was hailed to us as all-important. She spoke about it constantly, about how challenging it was to be a woman in the workplace, how hard she worked to get where she was. A career was expected of my father—of men in general—but what she did, oh, that was uncharted territory. She was really good at highlighting how essential her job was to her, so we expected it to override all her other responsibilities—including us.

We lived in a relatively large apartment in Manhattan, so it wasn't immediately clear that my parents were having issues because sound didn't travel well. But eventually my siblings and I caught on to the muted sounds of almost nightly arguments coming from my parents' room. My older sister takes after my mom—she never much cared about what was going on with other people; as long as she got what she wanted, she was fine. But I've always been more of an empath, more like my dad, and I wanted to know what they were fighting about. I took to roaming the halls after bedtime, hoping to overhear. And one night, I heard enough to piece together that my mom had been having an affair with her boss from work, whom I'd met many times before. I hate to say it because I love my father, but this guy was exactly the type of guy you'd expect my mom to be with.

No matter what might have been going on with my parents, they never let on to us kids that they were having problems. I didn't tell my sister and brother what I overheard—my brother was too young to understand, and I always had a sense that my sister would back my mom, that she would rationalize her behavior, and I didn't want to hear it. As the months went by, the arguments died down. I assumed that my mother had stopped the affair. She kept her same job, though, and as far as I knew he still worked with her, so I always worried (on my father's behalf) that things would heat back up. I've always been very partial to my father, and have always felt very protective of him, so finding out about the affair really soured me to my mother and bonded me even more to my dad. I had always sought my mother's acceptance and love, but the revelation about the affair made me want to antagonize her. I picked at her words, derided her choices, made her feel bad about how she'd mothered us, every chance I got.

One by one, the three of us left for college. During my junior year, my mother called me and told me she'd been diagnosed with breast cancer. I took some time off school and went back home to help take care of her (my brother and sister did not). Once I got home, though, it was my dad who struck me as worn down. He'd lost weight and seemed really tired, and he took me aside to give me instructions about her care. He said that she was insisting on working from home on the days that she felt up to it, which I found pretty typical of her. When I went in to see her, she seemed fine— in good spirits. She asked me about school and the boy I was dating, of whom she didn't approve, but what's new there . . . and then I went to my room to unpack.

The doorbell rang, and I went to answer it, but I saw that my dad was standing in the doorway, talking to my mom's boss from work (the guy she'd had an affair with all those years ago). And to my surprise, my dad motioned the guy in. He made his way to my parents' room and closed the door behind him. When I asked my dad what that was about, he said that it was work-related—they had some big project coming up.

I stayed home for about three months while she went through chemo, and her boss came to visit her several times a week. So, I gathered, the affair had never stopped. My dad just kept going about things, business as usual, bringing her meals to her in bed, fluffing her pillows—showing her fucking lover in.

I wanted nothing more than to confront her, but it hardly seemed like the right time. I kept my mouth shut and seethed when he visited her. Right before I was due to go back to school, though, I caught my dad alone in the kitchen. He was making her tea. I asked him straight out how long it had been going on, and he didn't act like he didn't know what I was talking about—he didn't insult my intelligence, which I've always appreciated about my dad, that he treated me like an adult worthy of respect. He confirmed that they'd been having an affair for six years—which means it had never stopped since I first discovered it all those years ago. I told him that I had overheard them arguing one night, and he said he figured I knew. I asked him how, and he said he'd noticed I had started giving my mother a hard time.

I left to finish up school, and my mother fully recovered. I got a job and an apartment about two hours away from the city, and although I spoke to my dad every week, I didn't visit home, hardly ever, and my mom and I all but cut ties. My dad and I got lunch in the city often, but I avoided her altogether. It was an unspoken thing, but she knew that I knew. I resented her for bulldozing over my father, for not appreciating him. He deserved to be with someone who loved him, not someone who treated him like a toy whose sheen had worn off.

I was at an event at my kid's kindergarten one day when my dad called to tell me that my mom had fallen and was in the ER due to a head injury. I asked him how he was holding up. Life had taught me to be more worried for him. He said he was all right but that she was asking for me. I said I'd try to make it but had no intention of going to see her. I hadn't seen her in years—she'd met my kid once, when he was born.

The event ended, and we went back home and had dinner. I was putting my son to bed when my cell phone rang again. It was my dad, telling me that my mom had passed away. I felt nothing at first (and I was surprised at how little I felt in terms of sadness or loss), and then I felt angry all over again because it felt like she'd had the last word.

My father told me at her funeral, by way of explanation, I guess, for the infidelity that he allowed in their marriage for all those years, that she was a strong woman and she was going to have life her way. "I was happy to be in it, to be part of the show," he said. "And I got you guys."

Her lover was at the funeral, too, by the way. I guess it was small consolation that he looked pretty grief-stricken, the poor sap.

So, about strong women. My mother lived the life she wanted to live, others be damned. I guess there's something to be admired about that, even if ours were the lives she destroyed.

Maggie, thirties

I went through a family album a few weeks ago and came across a photo of myself when I must have been no older than five or six. I'm sitting on our dining room table with a pencil in my hand, doing what was probably that night's homework. My mother is looking over my left shoulder; my grandmother, over my right.

I remember these scenes vividly. My mother's watchful eye, my grandmother's unforgiving one—it took hours to get through the simplest assignment. I wrote and rewrote the alphabet and numbers; I colored perfectly inside the lines; I learned poems by heart and rehearsed them in front of an audience of my grandmother's friends. Over time, I started taking pride in being, I guess, perfect.

Once, in second grade, I didn't get an A on an assignment and came home crying so hard that my mother, pitying me, decided against punishing me. Another time, I was playing in my parents' bedroom with a friend; we decided to climb the credenza that held their brand-new TV, toppling and shattering it on our way up. I was so afraid of the punishment that I hid under my parents' bed for the remainder of the night. They let me. I woke up the next morning with a sore neck from having slept on the cold floor.

I'm telling you this because these instances of me being less than a model daughter are so aberrant that they stand out like mountains in the otherwise flat topography of my childhood. My parents expected a lot. In their insistence that I be "the best"— whatever that might have meant in that particular moment—they discharged any concern they should have had with speaking unkindly. Over the years, I've internalized their language and now the unkind voice I hear in my head is no longer theirs.

When I turned sixteen, I developed an eating disorder. Bulimia, for me, was about punishment and control. I hated my body for being less than perfect, and I hated myself for being weak—for not having the discipline to work out and eat well so that I could have a perfect body—and so I started throwing up. It wasn't always after a binge. Sometimes, I'd decide that I'd eaten "too much"—the amount was arbitrary and mostly based on my emotional state at the moment—and so I'd throw up until my stomach felt empty. Other times, I'd empty out the kitchen and then spend an hour next to the toilet bowl with a gallon of water next to me, my index and middle fingers covered in vomit.

It's sick, how good it felt to throw up. I'd go into that bathroom feeling disgusting and leave feeling . . . perfect again. I felt like I'd kind of cheated the system, too. I could eat whatever I wanted and I had a shortcut to skinny. And the fact that I knew how much damage I must be doing to my body was just a bonus, because I felt that I deserved it. I felt deep, deep disappointment and shame in myself, in my eating disorder, in my messiness.

I was in my early twenties when I outgrew bulimia, but I never stopped equating my body image with my self-worth. When I am happy with myself, with my body, I am unstoppable. When I am not, I feel unworthy of love. And I can feel both of these things on the same day.

Bulimia was probably just a side effect of the issues I still battle as an adult, it's just that now the side effects aren't as readily identifiable. There's a point in most people's lives, I think, when they realize that their parents have really fucked them up. My moment came a few months ago. I'd started going to therapy to manage my anxiety and I was telling my therapist about how much trouble I have with the unknown, with not having control, with gray areas, with anything undefined—how much anxiety I feel every day, fueled by an ever-replenishing fear of failure. And it finally clicked for me that anxiety was my brain's response to the drill sergeant lodged inside my head, barking out expectations, directions, corrections. So I've replaced an eating disorder with an anxiety disorder. Progress: zero.

I came to these realizations pretty late in life because I thought that looking back into my childhood meant blaming my parents, and I didn't want to blame my parents. *Every unhappy family is unhappy in its own way*, right? There are so many ways to go wrong when starting a family and especially when raising children. I do believe that my parents did the best they could. Wait, that's not true. They could have divorced, but then that would probably have come with its own set of scars. So what's the point of the blame game?

I was talking to my mother the other day about my struggle with the stress in my life—I never call it anxiety when I'm talking to her because she'd rush to diminish it—and I told her that I learned from them that "imperfection needs to be punished." She demurred. "You didn't turn out so bad."

My parents' response to anything that could be construed as criticism about my childhood is to throw the fact that I'm a functioning adult in my face. And I guess to any outsider, I am. But I wake up every day feeling that my life is harder than it needs to be—and that I am to blame, that I do it to myself. My anxiety is crippling. Sometimes, I have trouble going out in public—just the thought of taking the train somewhere, for example, is totally overwhelming: *What if I miss the train? What if the cabbie tries to swindle me by taking a roundabout way? Will I get in everyone's way with all my bags? Am I standing in the wrong place?*

I have intrusive thoughts about terrible things happening, and so most nights I lie awake and torture myself with *what-if*s. If anything triggers me, I find a way to fit it into a narrative that proves that the worst-case scenario will happen. There are whole weeks that go by that I am so consumed by a thought—it seems that I think nothing *but* it. I wake up and it's the first thing I think. In the shower. It's what's preoccupying my thoughts on my way to work, in between emails and meetings, and at drinks. I have no break, no "off" switch, until I go to sleep. It seems that my fear stems from the thought that if I can't control the world around me, it will fall apart. The irony is that I can't even control my own thoughts.

Who would understand this besides my therapist? Well, in spite of our issues, my mom and I are close. My therapist says that we have a codependent relationship. I know that my mother certainly overdepends on me; I spent my childhood being her shrink. But whenever my back is to the wall and I need someplace to release a bit of steam, hers is the first number I dial. I must be suffering from memory loss because every time the phone rings, I have a sense of hope that maybe she'll say something to bring things into focus, to make me feel better. But inevitably, I hang up feeling disappointed, or worse. My mother has a way to turn the tables—to make you feel bad for her. So instead of getting a little bit of levity from my own burdens, I end up carrying some of hers, too.

This isn't new. I grew up witnessing my parents' imperfections so actively—they fought almost every single day when I was in my teens—that I internalized this fear that I'd become like my father. Like my father, because I identified him as the aggressor, the one in the wrong. And then, as I matured and started to understand the nuances of their relationship a little better, I started to become afraid that I'd turn out like my mother. So I ran in the other direction, railing against every personality trait that I identified as hers. As a result, I probably took on a little bit of each.

I wonder what would have happened had they just divorced. The thing about staying together for the kids is that you're forcing said kids to witness and internalize your shitty marriage. After hundreds, probably thousands of fights, my mother would come crying to me. "What do I do?" And I would tell her, "Leave him, you're not happy, leave him." Imagine saying that at twelve years old. Imagine having to barge into one of their fights to tell them that I could hear them from across the yard—that the neighbors could hear everything they were screaming at each other. And then seeing those neighbors the next day, their pitying eyes inevitably falling on me.

She never left, of course. And decades into their marriage, they're both still complaining about the same things that bothered them about each other when they were just married. Nothing has changed. They still treat us the same—with the same impossibly high standards, expecting that we put up with the dysfunction because of "familial duty." Because we owe them for raising us. For dressing us, feeding us, schooling us. If only that's all it took to raise a child—the expedient completion of the basic necessities. If only.

None of my siblings are married or have children yet. We focus on our careers. Our parents have given up on asking us about our personal lives altogether. It's a pleasant fantasy to think that they know that this is because of them—because each of us, in our own way, is tormented by the idea that we're doomed to repeat history. But they're probably oblivious. And my anxiety—my diligence, my micromanagement, my fear—I think that's me fighting the inertia that would inevitably lead me to becoming them entirely. It's me not wanting to repeat their history, their dysfunction.

So, career it is. I've picked something that is easy to lose myself in, something that can take over my whole life. And I let it. No, I *want* it to. I want my career to make me so busy, the static white noise of it to be so loud and overwhelming that it will drown out the emptiness everywhere else. No kids. No husband. No personal life. Just work. All work. And I'm good at my job. Fuck—I'm amazing at it. But—you get it—I have to be. Because then what am I without it? At work, I can control everything. I can micromanage. I can set unrealistic standards and challenge myself, and punish myself when I fall short. Which is fine, because perfectionism in my field is encouraged. So is single-mindedness. And being a female, having a family, having a life—all are obviously huge detractors.

And my siblings—all the same. Extremely successful in their respective fields. We have a pattern—we've all been molded by our childhoods in the same way. But we can't talk about these things. It's too painful to talk about with my siblings, and it's just impossible to talk about with my parents.

They would deflect—"You think we were raised better?"

My mind just went to what might happen if I had children. Scary.

They would judge. Belittle. Dismiss.

And if, by some extreme long shot, we would have persisted in demanding closure, my mother would break down crying. Game over. That's the trump card. The tears make me question my reality—am I making a big deal out of nothing? Am I blaming my parents for something that's my responsibility? Am I being too harsh?

So for the most part, the struggle is totally internal. I feel pretty damaged, but I guess most people do, anyways. I feel guilty because I feel like I've thrown my parents under the bus by complaining about them and my childhood—they did do the best they could in their circumstance. And look, we weren't hit. We weren't abused. They had high expectations, but isn't that a sign of caring? They always used to say, "We ask a lot of you because we see how much potential you have."

I don't know anymore—I go back and forth on it. One thing is for certain: I've become so afraid of losing that I'm no longer even playing the game. I've become so consumed by my anxiety, consumed by all that went wrong and the effect that it had on me, that I've stopped living.

Shelly, forties

I was sixteen when he raped me. I got pregnant, and my parents told me I had to marry him. My family were devout Jehovah's Witnesses—and everything in my life seemed very black-and-white. I knew what was expected of me, and there were many rules I had to adhere to. One of them was that there was no sex before marriage; another, that I was not allowed to have a boyfriend unless the intention was marriage. And obviously, I knew I had to date and marry someone of the same faith. So I really had no choice.

I remember the conversation with my father. He told me I should not have put myself in that situation, and that I had to marry Kevin. Abortion was not an option. I was still a Witness at the time, and I believed that abortion was an unforgivable act; I would lose out on everlasting life, and there would be no way to redeem myself.

So we went to the courthouse and got married. I stayed for two years, and I got pregnant again. I had my second child, and when she was six months old, I packed up my car in the middle of the night and I drove us all to a homeless women's shelter. And that was the first time in over two years that I felt I could breathe.

My parents didn't speak to me. I was excommunicated from our community and forbidden from contacting any of the members. I was completely alone—all the people I'd ever known and loved had banished me from their lives.

I stayed in the shelter for six months, and then a friend took us in for about a year. My mom reached out to me after that and asked to be a part of the kids' lives. We moved in with my parents for a few years, but my dad didn't speak to me—and hasn't since. It's been over fifteen years.

My ex was a very violent man. While we were married, he repeatedly beat me. I'd call my mom, and she would take the kids while I went to the hospital. She saw me like that—like a bruised stray animal, scared and in tatters—but she never asked me if I needed help. I put a restraining order against my ex when we were finalizing the divorce, and I guess it wasn't really a surprise when my mom came forward in court and claimed that she'd seen Kevin molest our oldest child.

Kevin ended up getting supervised visitation, but shortly after the divorce, he completely disappeared from our lives. He has only seen his kids once since then, and I obviously think it's for the best that he is kept away from my children. But I never made peace with what my mother said in court: if she did see my ex-husband molesting our son, then why hadn't she said anything earlier? I was tormented.

Was she lying now? In her twisted world, did she feel that she was finally doing something to help me and my children? On the other hand, she'd seen the way he beat me and she hadn't said anything about that, either. Was she trying to redeem herself by confessing something that would break open the family that she and my father had forced me into?

I don't know. My gut tells me not to trust her. She believes in the Bible above all, yet she turns a blind eye when someone is hurting her daughter—her own blood. This seems so contradictory, so twisted. She told me to stay with Kevin and God would reward me for my pain and suffering when I returned in the new life. But why is it not okay for me to leave someone who hurts me? And why does the Bible trump the welfare of your own child?

I've been excommunicated from Kingdom Hall, and I can't speak to any of the members; technically, that includes my parents. I think they wouldn't have taken me in had I not had children—they felt sympathy for the kids. Everyone was complicit in covering up the rape and pretending everything was okay. My parents can never acknowledge that they did anything wrong. When I discuss things with my mother, she says, "We did the best we could, and we tried to follow the Bible."

As for me, I need to make good with God before I'll be accepted into Kingdom Hall and their lives again.

I thought that after everything happened, I was finally free of them. But unfortunately, when my son was five years old, he was diagnosed with ADHD. At ten, I noticed that he was talking to things and people who weren't there. I took him in to get evaluated, and he was diagnosed with bipolar disorder and schizophrenia. He was put on medication and was doing really well, but as he grew older, he became medication noncompliant. When he wasn't on his medication, he attacked me and his sister, and it became increasingly difficult for us to not fear him.

I looked up a six-month program that helps adolescents struggling with behavioral issues. My son would have left the program with mentors, job opportunities, and a support system to help him during difficult times. I sat down with my parents and explained my plan—told my father that I was afraid my son would hurt someone and I wanted to protect my daughter. My mother has always had a really close relationship with my son—I've always thought it bordered on unhealthy. She kind of acted like she was his wife, like she weirdly idolized him. My son could do no wrong—she would do anything for him.

Her response was, "If you take him from me, I won't be able to live anymore."

I was at work one day shortly thereafter when I was served with a restraining order—she'd filed it to keep me away from my son. After a court battle and a lot of money spent on lawyers, the order was dropped. However, my son went missing. For eight months, I couldn't find him. My mother was in cahoots with one of my sisters and Kevin to keep him away from me. Kevin—who was abusive. Kevin—who she claimed molested my son. And she said she did it because she wanted to protect my son from *me*.

I was heartbroken and asked her about the allegations again, and about how she could send my son to live with Kevin when she claimed in court that he had molested him. She said, "I don't remember saying that." I asked her about Kevin beating me, about her keeping the kids when I went to the hospital for treatment. She "didn't remember" that, either.

When my son finally came back to me, he was angry. He tried to commit suicide, and under my mother's influence, he refused treatment for his mental illness. She claims that all he has to do is go to Kingdom Hall—some of the more devout JWs don't believe in taking medication. My parents believe that prayer will make my son better and when he returns in the new life, he will return with no ailments. They don't believe in the justice system, in voting, in modern health care—they believe that this was Judas's arrangement, and that God is not "of the world," so worldly solutions are not for his people. Only he can help them.

Jehovah's Witnesses are led by "the Society"—a group of men who have been handpicked by God to lead them. These men don't believe that women should be educated. They believe that we should dedicate 100 percent of our lives to serving God, finding a man, getting married, and having babies. If you go to school, you're serving the world, you're not serving God. They don't want people to waste their time on efforts that mean nothing because "you never know when Armageddon will come."

The best thing I did in my life was to leave. But my mother has her claws into my son, they're dragging him into these beliefs—they're brainwashing him against me and deeper into their community. I worked so hard to get away, only to feel like I'm regressing.

It feels like it's been a lifetime since everything happened, but also like my struggle is not over yet. I got my GED, then I went to college, and then I put myself through grad school. It seems like I should be a different person, like I should move on. But I can't—I yearn for my parents to tell me that they were wrong, to acknowledge the effect that their decision had on my life. I yearn for them to see me as their child and not some foreign object, some pariah.

I could have been so much more. My life could have been so different. I could maybe wake up every morning not feeling that I am broken, that I am unwanted, that I am a victim, that I am less than, that my existence is futile, that I am a liar and a fake. I wonder what it would be like to feel comfortable—to feel that my soul has settled. I live in the shadow of what I wish my life had been.

I wonder what it's like to trust people, too. I trust no one. It's hard to get close to people and to experience joy, but I've known nothing different. "I love you" means nothing to me—they're just words that are tossed around casually. I think that it's naive and gullible to believe that people are good. I don't think they are—I think people's morality and goodness is totally circumstantial and mercurial. At the end of the day, I think the only God people serve is the self.

I've lied to my own kids, and that's hard to come to terms with. I can't tell them that their dad beat and raped me. I can't tell my daughter, so I tell her that her dad and I didn't get along. How would she feel if she knew that she was a product of rape? She doesn't even know that I didn't even walk in my graduation ceremony. She's graduating from high school herself this weekend and she asked me about my diploma. I had to lie to her—again. I think about her and how much I love her, and then I think about my relationship with my own parents. If, God forbid, anything ever happened to her, I could never harden my heart to her, I could never tell her that rape was ever her fault.

And what will my children think of me when I eventually tell them about my past? What will they think of their grandparents? How will they view the world when something they'd taken for granted—that they were the product of a consensual relationship—turns into the ugly truth? I don't know what that does to young adults, and I don't know how it disfigures their future. But I know that I don't want to do to my kids what my parents did to me—I don't want to be the reason for their unhappiness.

Elsa, midfifties

My day is pretty intense in the sense that it doesn't really have a beginning or end. I don't sleep like a typical person might—from whatever time at night, until her alarm rings in the morning. I am always on call, always ready. Every part of my day is measured—every minute, and I have to be very efficient in order to get it all done. So I don't have time to process anything, and that's probably for the best. I go, go, go, and I don't give it time to seep in, what I'm going through.

I was eight months pregnant with my daughter when we moved to the United States—gosh, it's hard to believe that was over twenty years ago now. My son, Marcus, who was four at the time, and I moved here for the same reason most immigrants do—for a better life. My husband stayed behind and worked, planning to join us once I'd had Chelsea. I'd been here for three weeks when I went to my ob-gyn appointment one morning, and he told me I was in labor and I needed to go to the hospital to deliver. "No, I'm not," I told him. I wasn't having contractions. I'd been through unmedicated labor with Marcus, and I still vividly remembered the pain. But sure enough, my water broke on the bus on the way there.

It was the most horrific feeling—being alone with my son, in labor, on a bus, having no idea where we were going or whom to trust for help. I reluctantly called my sister-in-law—we've never had the best relationship and I had been staying in her home, which was a nightmare. I asked her to meet me at the hospital, where the OB on call was telling me I'd have to sit down—"Let us take care of you now," he kept saying. But I was so on guard, so used to taking care of myself—being the responsible one, the one in charge, in control—that I couldn't let go. I couldn't relax.

When Chelsea finally came, she had the cord wrapped around

her neck, so she didn't cry right away, and she was blue. But she was fine, and I was grateful that the delivery, at least, had been uncomplicated. When Marcus and I left the hospital, I remember clutching his hand and pushing Chelsea's bassinet with the other. And I prayed to God, I said: "Please God, help me. Help me raise these children in this strange land, all by myself."

When she was four weeks old, Chelsea caught a virus. The doctor who helped us at the hospital was Greek, and she told me that her parents had come to America just like I had—alone, with nothing. And she said, "Both my brother and I are doctors now. Your children will be just fine. You are strong." I remember everything about her—her name, her features, her words. I want to look her up, just to tell her how grateful I am for her help.

My husband didn't end up joining us for another three months. In the meantime, we moved out of my sister-in-law's apartment and to the Bronx. It was even more obvious there that we were foreigners with nothing but hopes. No papers. No job. The apartment was a tiny one-bedroom in a gloomy six-story building where the elevator smelled like urine and the neighbors were, generally, far from friendly. But my immediate next-door neighbor was a sweet older lady. She gave me her grandson's bed for Chelsea to sleep in, and Marcus and I slept on a mattress that we'd found on the street. We had very little other furniture. Every night, though, my neighbor would come to the apartment and talk to me, give me advice, tell me about her life. In those five months that she lived there, I learned so much. She got me through those days. She gave me hope.

When my husband finally came—Chelsea must have been about four months old—life was hard until we got papers. He was a philosophy professor back home, and he worked as a bartender in the Bronx. I went back to school when I was thirty-nine and I got my master's degree in engineering. I worked a temp job as an accountant and a few other part-time gigs, went to school at night, and then when I got home, my husband would take the night shift at the bar. For two years, we only saw each other long enough to hand off the children. In a sense, we always thought that if we couldn't achieve anything in five years, we would have considered it a wash and gone back. But after I got my master's, I almost immediately got a job as a structural engineer. Then, it was my husband's turn to go to school—he got his paralegal degree, and eventually we felt financially secure. Life got a little bit easier, and we were actually living, instead of just surviving. We put in our time in the Bronx and then bought a house in a great neighborhood in the suburbs.

Almost right after we bought the house in 2011, my husband was diagnosed with stomach cancer. We were at the doctor's office, and he was totally stone-faced when he got the news. I was crying. I couldn't understand the implications—my brain had trouble wrapping itself around the situation—and the word itself just seemed so harsh. *Cancer.* The disease was hard to endure—the concept of it, and the treatment.

These are the things that I'll never forget: going to the hospital every day after work, being with him in the room, trying to protect the children from the worst of it. And we were alone—no close family to lean on. Marcus was graduating from high school, Chelsea from middle school. The kids still needed us so much, and my brain had to contend with—*What if he dies? What will I do? What will the kids do?* But my husband was very strong all through chemo and surgery. What happened, though, is that it took years to be in the clear, to beat it, and it took him over mentally. It was a Pyrrhic victory. Physically, he recovered. But mentally, he was never the same.

It must have been around 2014 when I started putting it together. I noticed little things, little lapses that were easy to justify at first. Maybe he doesn't remember X because he's just never paid attention to these things. But he also seemed a little dull, expressionless. And he was forgetting things—he wasn't sharp anymore.

We were on vacation. We were taking this tunnel from Northern Italy to Austria. It was the most beautiful thing I'd ever seen—just breathtaking scenery all around. I was driving, and my husband was in the front seat with me. The kids were in the back, along with a cousin of my husband who worked with geriatric populations in Austria. She kept looking at him, watching him. And we both noticed that his affect, his eyes, were totally flat—like he wasn't receiving any information. His cousin pulled me aside later and said, "I don't like the way he looks." She was the first one, as an outsider, to point out that something was happening.

My husband kept going to work, but it was obvious that whatever was happening to him, it was progressing quickly. I knew these types of degenerative neurological diseases just get worse with time, so I wasn't optimistic. I was also in denial—part of me didn't really *want* to know what was happening. They kept him at work out of loyalty. He had been there for fifteen years—an exemplary employee. With time, though, he was losing the ability to complete even the simplest tasks. He couldn't fill in his time sheet or log in to his computer. He began getting lost on the train on the way to work and I would get panicked calls from him—*I'm lost, I don't know where I am.*

One day, this past January, he had gotten off at his usual stop and couldn't find his office. So he kept going around and around the block, in the middle of the freezing winter, for four hours. One of his colleagues had left the building to go to lunch and ran into him on the street. And that was his last day at work. After that, we went to many doctor's offices until we found one who had an answer for us: posterior cortical atrophy, brought on by the cancer. And there were other diseases at play, too—dementia, Alzheimer's—diseases that affect everything: his eyes, memory, logic. It has taken everything from him. He is a vacant shell.

It's been eight years of this. Eight years of keeping it together. I wake up many times at night because he can't find the door if he needs to go to the bathroom. He gets out of bed and stands against the wall until I take him by the hand. My alarm finally rings at 6:00 a.m., and I start by telling him that he needs to shave. Sometimes, he shaves and then he does it a second time because he's forgotten. I wash him. I dress him. He hangs around—usually just sits on the bed—and watches me get ready. We go downstairs together and I turn on the TV for him, and then I give him something to eat. I have to cut up his food into bite-size pieces. After, I give him his medication. Then, someone comes to pick him up and drop him off at the adult day care center, and I leave for work.

At work, I go to meetings, take calls. I manage at least four or five projects at any particular time, and most of my days are nine or ten hours long. I always work through lunch. It's not the type of job that you walk out of the building and be finished—I take work home with me. My job as a structural engineer is particularly important because I have to essentially make sure that a building will stand; I design its skeleton, its backbone. Any mistake is potentially fatal at worst, or hugely costly at best.

At the end of my day, I pick my husband up from the center. This last week, I found him in tears. I gathered from what he was saying that he'd been crying because he thought I'd been in a car accident and died. He's deeply unhappy at the center, but I have exhausted my options. I used to have an aide come to our home to care for him. He couldn't handle that because he became paranoid and saw her as a threat, as a foreigner who was trying to steal from him. I came home one day and she was in tears—he'd gotten agitated and hit her. But when he was telling me what had happened, it was the aide who had hit him.

Once I'm home, I have to pay the mortgage, pay for both of my kids' school loans, pay to put food on the table. I have to communicate with medical insurance, which is so, so tiresome. There's a nonprofit that's helping me to coordinate the documents that are required, but the paperwork is still endless. Every penny of what I make has to be accounted for, and anything "extra" is garnished to pay for my husband's medical bills. It took me more than a year to figure out how the system works—who pays for what. It's a full-time job in and of itself because it's a bureaucratic system that puts a lot of pressure on the caretaker, *me*. In my spare time, I am the plumber, the handywoman, the maid, the cook, the finance person. For everything, the buck stops with me.

It's a curse, what's happening to us. And I feel very responsible for keeping it from affecting the kids.

My son is well out of college; he has a great job and lives with his girlfriend. He is not as invested as we are because he's not around now. But even when he was living at home, he lived in his own space, emotionally. That's how he tried to protect himself, by being kind of aloof. Chelsea thinks that he's not compassionate. She just graduated from college, and she lives at home for now. She's only been here for three months, but she is struggling a lot. I've noticed that, to console herself, she goes online and reads what other people say about this sort of disease and how they handle it. Often, what she finds is upsetting. We differ in that I don't feel like I need a support group. Other people's stories don't help me with my everyday life. I don't have the time to stop and internalize what's happening, and that's how I cope. I find myself to be, mentally, very strong. Chelsea is young, and she is struggling to accept what has happened to her father. She has a lot of emotional breakdowns, and I don't know how to console her. I suffer the same way, but I hide it better. I have been able to keep it to myself. I can't even cry. It's been a long time of keeping it together.

I don't know what's saving me. Maybe a bright hope? I've always believed that tomorrow will be better than today, but I don't know what that looks like, for us. I feel that my energies are waning. I give and give, and I have to dig deep within that inner well to find the strength I need to make it through every day. But I fear that one day I'll reach the bottom—I'll find that I've run out of strength. What will happen then? Of course, I can't dwell on that for too long. I have to move forward. That's what makes life beautiful: all the obstacles and curveballs you're thrown, everything you've worked hard to achieve, all the strength you've mustered to go on when you didn't think it possible. Sometimes, when you look back, it looks like you've made a real mess of things. But you have to accept everything as part of the beauty of being human. In a sense, it all turns to gold.

Helena, thirty

I didn't sleep at all in the hospital bed the night before Ronan was born. They'd hooked up a monitor to my belly, and his heartbeat echoed throughout the room. My breath would catch with every single flutter of his heart. I couldn't wrap my head around it—that he would be here soon, that we would be a family of three. When he was born and they plopped him on my chest, I think I was in a state of shock that gave way to delirium. When I wasn't trying to feed him, I was watching him sleep in his little bassinet, never more than a few inches away from me. And even though I was exhausted and in tremendous pain, I couldn't sleep. I felt like I needed to protect him, to watch him constantly.

They kept us in the hospital an extra day because I was Group B Strep positive, and I had been induced due to a high leak in my placenta. Although Ronan had gotten a full course of antibiotics, they wanted to monitor him. I felt like my body had failed, like I had put my son in danger. So I felt a tremendous responsibility to never abandon my post—to always keep a watchful and protective eye. But I was struggling.

My milk hadn't come in, and Ronan was a sleepy one. He wasn't getting much to drink—he couldn't latch—and in a panic, I told our nurses that we needed to supplement him with formula. Instead, a lactation consultant came to talk to us and spent about five minutes going over the basics of feeding. She gave me a nipple shield and told me to keep trying, and whoosh, was gone. I wasn't being heard—try as I did, I was sure that Ronan wasn't getting any colostrum. I pumped and pumped for hours at a time and nothing came out.

The day that we were supposed to get discharged, my husband, Alex, brought in the stroller, and we put Ronan in its bassinet. Against the pristine (twice-washed) bassinet cover, he looked . . . yellow. I called in the nurse and told her as much, but she quickly dismissed it. I persisted.

"Well, there's no harm in checking again," she conceded, and went off to get the apparatus that checks the skin for jaundice. And sure enough, the test showed that he was in intermediate-high risk. We were discharged nonetheless and told to check in the next day with his pediatrician.

At the pediatrician's, the blood test showed high bilirubin levels. We were told to get him back to the pediatric ER, where he would be processed and then put into this glass incubator that emitted the equivalent of the sun's UV rays. As I understood it, these would help Ronan's liver "burn off" the bilirubin. There was another mom with a "bili baby" in the bed next to ours. She came in a few hours after us, and I could hear her crying into the night. Alex and I slept on a hardwood "bed" not much wider than a park bench, next to Ronan's incubator. In the meantime, I pumped. And then I pumped. And then I pumped some more. And in my gut, I knew that he was jaundiced because he hadn't gotten enough to eat. Because I had failed him. Again. And he was only four days old.

But his bilirubin levels did come down, and we were discharged the next day with express instructions to check back in two days. We went back to the doctor's office with a lightness in our step, happy to put the last few days behind us. The follow-up news wasn't good, though—his numbers had increased. His liver wasn't burning off the bilirubin, and I charged myself with figuring out why. I read everything I could get my hands on—articles about rare diseases, about the effects of high bilirubin on a baby's brain, an article by a mother who, much like me, had been ignored when she'd asked to supplement her baby with formula. The baby had become jaundiced, lost a lot of weight, and was now a toddler with severe physical and developmental delays.

You should have insisted, my brain told me. *You should have fed your child. You should have listened to your gut. You didn't protect him.*

My husband, a doctor, tried his best to convince me that our son's liver just hadn't matured yet. I'd been induced, likely before Ronan was ready to meet us. And so we just needed to be patient.

But all I could see was his skin. I convinced myself, with each passing minute, that he was either getting more yellow, or less yellow. It was a terrible seesaw—I distrusted my brain, my eyes. In every moment of the day, I was solely preoccupied with Ronan and the color of his skin and eyes. When we went back to his pediatrician's office to recheck his numbers, they told us they had risen again. Risk averse, the pediatrician sent us back to the pediatric ER.

I was in shambles. My hands shook as I paced the waiting room, my mind wandering to everything that I'd read that could be wrong. Finally, the pediatric ER doctors consulted a gastroenterologist, who consulted a hematologist at a different hospital who, without laying an eye on our son, told us that we should put our ten-day-old on phenobarbital, a serious anti-seizure medication that had been used to lower bilirubin in infants in the 1960s. My husband was livid. He pushed the doctor for answers—answers she didn't have. She was just the messenger. "You can always leave and not give him the medication," she said with a disinterested shrug.

And that's what we did. Over the next several weeks, we went back to the pediatrician and had Ronan's heel poked, his blood taken, and his bili levels checked. I supplemented him with formula while I pumped day and night to get my milk supply up. I didn't sleep. I didn't think about anything but my son. And whenever our cell phone rang—the doctor calling to let us know the results—I felt a fear so overwhelming that it was unlike anything I'd ever experienced before. I would hide in the next room, my hands over my ears, my head in between my knees, and rock myself back and forth until the call was over. Sometimes I could hear Alex "whoop" in the next room, and I knew the number had come down. Other times, it was the elated look on his face—over two weeks it was obvious that

Ronan's bilirubin was coming down. His color got better. My husband told me he was happy to finally be putting this behind us. My mom was relieved, too.

But while my mom was in the kitchen, while Ronan slept, while Alex showered, I went online and looked at the *what-ifs*. *What if he has brain damage? What if we waited too long to feed him? What if he can never run, never play soccer? Alex always dreamed of playing soccer with Ronan. And I took that away from him. It is my fault.*

Once the bilirubin scare passed, my brain frantically sought the next thing to worry about. Until Ronan was six months old, I was convinced that he had cerebral palsy. I looked at the way that he used his hands and feet—unevenly, I convinced myself—and was certain that his jaundice had caused it. And when I managed to dodge that fear for a few minutes, I began to wonder: *Well, if he is using his arms unevenly and if it isn't due to CP, what else could it mean?* So I googled it and found a study that showed a connection between movement disturbances and autism. A connection between head lag and autism. A connection between . . . anything . . . and autism. And when it wasn't CP or autism, it was something, anything else—meningitis, measles, cancer, IgA nephropathy, cold sores—and its accompanying rationale. Meningitis, because Alex works in a hospital and he brings home germs. Measles, because there's a measles outbreak in New York, and we live next to a hospital. Cancer, because I'm overusing Purell and children who are not introduced to viruses and bacteria enough as babies have higher incidence of childhood cancer. IgA nephropathy, because it runs in the family. Cold sores, because everyone has them and could unknowingly pass them on to my baby.

And even though my brain understood what was happening— that my anxiety warped my thinking, that I saw everything through an incredibly cloudy and unhealthy lens—I still could not help it. I could not help it enough to make a difference in my quality of life. And even now, it is uncomfortable. It is scary. Because I feel that I could be dragged right back down to that hell at any moment. People close to me, people who should have known better, told me to "get over it." They told me to get on medication because I was "not normal." Told me that I was doing motherhood wrong—that *they* had done it a certain way, and it was good enough for them. Did I think I was better than them?

When I saw the effect that I was having on Alex, who started crying one night when he asked me if I was suicidal—"I'm sorry, I have to ask"—I began to feel really, really lousy about myself. I began to feel that I was hurting my son by being sick like this, that I was dragging my husband down with my dysfunction. I began to hate myself for it.

So, yes, I did think about suicide. And then I thought about my husband, whom I love with all my heart, and I thought about what would happen to him if I went through with it. And I resolved to stay and get better, because I cannot fathom a world in which I cause him pain.

In the midst of this, I sought therapy. I called my ob-gyn and was referred to a center uptown that deals specifically with postpartum issues. My therapist there was awful—borderline unethical. She canceled more than half our appointments at the last minute, and told me (several sessions in) that she was actually still waiting for her license to practice and shouldn't charge me for sessions. When I emailed her to break off our relationship, she told me that it was just as well because she'd been thinking a lot about me, and "that's often not a good sign." She felt that a "higher level of care" was needed. Of course, that sent me into a panic. Was I losing my mind? Was this psychosis? Was I really doing so poorly that a doctor specializing in postpartum issues couldn't help me?

In that flurry of fear, I got another referral. When I called the office, I was told that the wait to see the doctor was six months. Six months. In New York City. In 2018.

But I did finally luck out. I found a lovely psychologist whom I learned to trust. And we started working on me, which felt good. Hard, but good. And then my husband's employer switched insurance, which landed me out of network for my doctor. And even though she petitioned to join, it has now been over five months without word. Five months without access to my therapist.

I know how lucky I am. I am lucky to live where I do. I am lucky because my husband is a doctor, so we are more medically literate than the average person. I am lucky because we are not poor, or uneducated. And yet I can't help but be shocked at how difficult it was for me to get postpartum mental health care. If this was my experience, I fear how much harder, still, it must be for women who don't have the same as privileges as I do.

The last few months have been an unraveling. A violent tug at the tapestry of me, of everything I thought I was as a person. My son's birth has felt like a sort of comeuppance—like payback for thinking that I had it together. *I am not strong. I am not rational. I am not a good mother; did I make a mistake in becoming one? Maybe I don't have the constitution for motherhood.* These thoughts are sad and scary to me, and I think them far too often, still. The worst part is that I can't trust myself, my own eyes: Ronan is thriving. He is a curious kid who loves the world and brings us so much happiness. And yet I can't relax—can't accept it. I question my own reality. Why is it that I feel the need to self-sabotage?

But the hardest times teach us the best lessons. I have learned to zoom out, to let go a little. To focus on what I can control. To simplify instead of complicate. To breathe through the fear. To cope with my anxiety as best I can. To accept that I am not a perfect human, and I cannot and will not be a perfect mother. To become comfortable in discomfort, in the new normal. To be kind to myself, especially when I feel undeserving, and to stop holding myself to unrealistic standards.

Everything is not perfect. But knowing that I'm not in it alone makes it, strangely, bearable. I guess it's only fitting that, after listening to the troubles of others, I finally learn this lesson myself. I imagine us all huddling together in a storm shelter, waiting for bad weather to pass. And pass it shall. How wonderful it is, to be human.

Acknowledgments

I'd like to thank Paul Smalera, my first editor at *Quartz* and the second person I ever told about *Craigslist Confessional*, for his kindness, guidance, and patience, and for giving me the space I needed to make something of this. My thanks to Jason Sacca, who was a really good sport about getting twenty emails a week, every week.

My gratitude, always, to my agent, Jeff Kleinman, for convincing me that *no*, I can't finish a book in six months postpartum, and for his tenacity, kindness, and generosity.

I tell her this all the time but for Rebecca Strobel, my editor, written gratitude is in order: I am so lucky we picked each other. My deepest thank you to my wonderful publisher, Jennifer Bergstrom, for her enthusiasm and vision. And to my incomparable team at Gallery Books: Aimée Bell, Jennifer Long, Sally Marvin, Lisa Litwack, John Vairo, Caroline Pallotta, John Paul Jones, Kaitlyn Snowden, and Davina Mock—thank you for working so hard to pull this together, and believing in the importance of telling these stories. And finally, to Sydney Morris, my publicist, and Bianca Salvant, my marketing specialist: thank you for making sure these stories found their kindred spirits.

Thanks to Erblin, for being a true friend, even though for a while there, he was convinced I'd lost my mind; and to Henry, for being the consummate host and a pretty stellar human being.

Mom and Dad—where do I begin? For their sacrifice, strength, and selflessness, I owe them everything.

And to my husband, Alex. You are my whole heart. Thank you for believing in me.

About the Author

Helena Dea Bala emigrated to the United States as a child. To make ends meet during those difficult first years, she helped her mother clean houses on the weekends. She graduated Phi Beta Kappa from George Washington University and worked to become a lawyer and lobbyist in Washington, DC. After her day job left her feeling disconnected and unfulfilled, she deferred her student loans, applied for a credit card, and gave herself one year—one year to just listen. Five years in, she now does Craigslist Confessional full-time. Find out more at craigslistconfessional.com.